GW00871583

DOING BUSINESS IN
BULGARIA

|CBI|
Initiative Eastern Europe

DOING BUSINESS IN
BULGARIA

TOUCHE ROSS
SINCLAIR ROCHE & TEMPERLEY
BRITISH GAS

KOGAN
PAGE

Note: This book has been written on the basis of information and law current as at September 1992.

First published in 1993

Kogan Page Limited
120 Pentonville Road
London N1 9JN

British Library Cataloguing in Publication Data

A CIP record for this book is available from the British Library.

ISBN 0 7494 0689 5

Typeset by DP Photosetting, Aylesbury, Bucks
Printed in England by Clays Ltd., St Ives plc.

Contents

PART III: THE OPTIONS FOR BRITISH BUSINESS   139

The Contributors

Sinclair Roche & Temperley is a leading international commercial law firm based in London, with offices in Hong Kong, Singapore and Bucharest and a presence in both Oslo and Ho Chi Minh City. The firm has acted for Bulgarian clients for over 30 years and has developed an in-depth understanding of the country and its changing political and business philosophy. Following the recent transition from a command to a free market economy in Bulgaria, Sinclair Roche & Temperley has forged close links with governmental agencies, legal advisers and professional consultants, essential in providing a business service to clients investing in the country. The firm has been involved in a number of joint ventures, financing transactions and other projects involving foreign investment in Bulgaria and hopes to use there the privatisation experience gained elsewhere in Central and Eastern Europe, once the Bulgarian Privatisation Programme begins in earnest.

Touche Ross & Co and the **Deloitte & Touche** practice in Bulgaria are part of Deloitte Touche Tohmatsu International, one of the world's largest accounting, auditing, tax and management consulting firms. The firm has extensive experience of assisting Western clients entering the Bulgarian market by providing advice on many areas including joint ventures, valuations, personnel, government relations, environmental factors, IT and customs software applications. Other major assignments include advising the Bulgarian Government on its Electricity Privatisation Programme, and also taking the lead role in the redevelopment of the telecommunications market in the country. Deloitte Touche Tohmatsu International has offices in all the major Central and Eastern European capitals, including Sofia, staffed by both Western and national professionals.

Touche Ross & Co would like to acknowledge the invaluable assistance of the Scientific Institute for International Cooperation and Foreign Economic Activities in Sofia in preparing many of the chapters contributed to this book.

SG Warburg is a leading international investment bank. Since the end of 1989, SG Warburg has been active in Eastern Europe where it has advised on projects in the former Eastern Germany, Poland, the Commonwealth of Independent States, Hungary and Czechoslovakia. In Bulgaria, SG Warburg is involved in a number of initiatives and since mid-1992, it has been advising Balkan Bulgarian Airlines on its privatisation.

British Gas is a world class energy company and leading international gas business.

Its principal activity is the purchase, distribution and sale of natural gas to domestic, industrial and commercial customers in Great Britain. The Company has a major hydrocarbon exploration and production division operating offshore and onshore; both in Great Britain and overseas. The Company also has an interest in gas-related activities across the world through its Global Gas business. British Gas is therefore a company concerned with all aspects of gas supply.

Through its Exploration and Production Business Unit, the Company is currently involved in a major expansion of its exploration and production activities in the UK and overseas, in oil as well as gas. In a short period it has established itself in ventures in over 20 countries spread across Europe, Africa, Asia and the Americas. This rapid growth is being built on a foundation of 30 years' experience in production and exploration in the UK and efforts will be focused in the future on developing this expertise worldwide.

Cerrex Ltd is a small London-based consultancy operating mainly in the fields of trade policy, government relations and export promotion and specialising in the newly emerging opportunities in Eastern Europe. It has undertaken a wide range of research on those markets and is currently planning to produce the first annual Eastern European Directories on electronics, energy and food processing in early-1993. The company has a network of contacts throughout the area.

Foreword

With this new book the CBI Initiative Eastern Europe offers the reader a volume of timely business information on the relatively small country of Bulgaria.

The Bulgarians are now re-embracing values that were once typical but were consigned to oblivion during 45 years of communist rule. Before getting to know the taste of democracy, people used to live in the unreal world of the centrally-planned economy. Now, in Bulgaria as in the other countries of Eastern Europe, people are painfully swallowing the slow pace of reforms. There are difficulties along the way as well as disappointment at the time needed to reach a Western standard of living.

We are carrying out a transition without precedent in human history. We are sailing in unknown waters. However, the drive to establish a free market in Bulgaria is a guarantee for the people's future.

Our economic philosophy rests on the establishment of a dynamic private sector and on export orientation towards the advanced market economies. This is the core of a long-term strategy which is aimed not only at trade expansion, but also at building up the requisite production base.

The collapse of traditional CMEA (or Comecon) markets dealt a heavy blow to our economy and made it imperative for us to look for new options by restructuring production and searching for new markets. This is a tall order, especially at this juncture when protectionism appears to be gaining pre-eminence over free trade and there is a growing tendency to set up regional trade blocs. I believe in our ability to make a breakthrough in exports, as long as we identify appropriate export niches for industrial products. This is particularly important now when we are witnessing an expansion of our exports to the 24 OECD countries and a very large percentage increase of our exports to the EC.

At the same time we are rebuilding the traditions in our business relations with the countries of the former Soviet Union and Eastern Europe. The lesson we have learnt is that only by relying on the diversity of our foreign economic relations can we combat the adverse consequences of the market situation. At present, we are witnessing a move from exploration of opportunities to concrete action.

There is no doubt, however, that the influx of foreign investment is the main catalyst for the advancement of the Bulgarian economy through improvements in organisation, the introduction of know-how and modern management practices, and access to new markets.

To attract more capital from abroad, we are relying on a new law for promotion of foreign investments, on political stability, and on the development of specific incentive mechanisms to encourage foreign companies to set up joint small and medium-sized private enterprises.

We want to attract people who are interested in medium and long-term investment, as well as sources of consultancy and technical assistance. Investors will be helped by the new privatisation and banking laws, which provide a framework for a system of private enterprise. Apart from a liberal law for the promotion of foreign investments, we are relying also on: our geographical location as a bridge between the markets of Western Europe, the former Soviet Union and the Middle and Far East; our inexpensive though well-educated and well-trained work-force; our traditions in agriculture, tourism, textile, food processing, high-quality tobacco products and vintage wines; our untapped production capabilities in electronics, chemicals, pharmaceuticals and machine-building; the expertise of our software experts; and our innate, unfading interest in all developments taking place in the rest of the world. I hope that today investors will see Bulgaria as Eastern Europe's new frontier of economic growth.

Filip Dimitrov
Prime Minister
of the Republic of Bulgaria
November 1992

Preface

Since early 1991 Bulgaria has pursued a wide-ranging strategy for creating a market economy and re-integrating itself into the world economy. While the scale of this task cannot be underestimated, progress is being made: prices have been freed, there is a liberal foreign investment law, privatisation has been set in train, an association agreement with the EC is in place and a new private sector is developing. As the country undergoes this period of rapid economic adjustment, different areas for business development are progressively opening up.

Bulgaria has a range of specialised activities worth attention, from wine and tobacco to fork-lift trucks and robotics. Other opportunities will arise in areas where Bulgaria needs to bring its standards up to an international level, either in the form of equipment or know-how. The potential for contracts is being strengthened by large amounts of international economic aid. Perhaps Bulgaria's greatest asset is its people with a high skill-to-wage ratio. Nor should the consumer market be dismissed. As elsewhere in the region there is an emerging segment of the population with real spending power.

This book is designed to provide companies with a practical guide to the emerging commercial framework and a breakdown of the opportunities for trade and investment. It draws principally on the experience and expertise of British Gas, Sinclair Roche & Temperley, Touche Ross and SG Warburg & Co. There have also been significant contributions from other people and companies active in the Bulgarian market: Michael Bird of Cerrex Ltd, Barbara Page Roberts of PR Trading, Brian Cole of East European Projects Consultants, Margarit Todorov of Domaine Boyar, Rod Allen of ICL and the country sales managers from Racal Recorders. The CBI thanks all these contributors for the substantial efforts they have made in making this book possible.

I am particularly glad that this book is being launched at the same time as the new British Bulgarian Chamber of Commerce in London. As a result I hope that more companies will be encouraged to look seriously at developing business in the emerging market of Bulgaria.

Alan J Lewis, CBE
Chairman, CBI Initiative Eastern Europe
December 1992

Part I

A Business Revolution?

1

Political and Legal Transformation

Sinclair Roche & Temperley

Bulgaria was once the most loyal supporter of the Soviet Union, often referred to as its 'sixteenth republic'. However, all this has now changed with the adoption of a new Constitution and the end of the old one-party system. With the former communist leader Todor Zhivkov serving a seven-year sentence for embezzlement and the former party headquarters in Sofia housing a cinema, the country is now established on the road to democracy and free enterprise.

HISTORICAL BACKGROUND

The modern Bulgarian state dates from the Treaty of San Stefano in 1878 when the country was liberated from five centuries of domination by the Ottoman Empire. Bulgaria sided with Germany in World Wars I and II, and suffered badly in both with crippling inflation and food shortages leading to low morale among the troops and the civilian population. In late 1944, with Soviet victory looking assured on the eastern front and with the Red Army massing on Bulgaria's northern frontier, Sofia severed its political and military ties with Germany. In September 1944, the 'Fatherland Front' staged a successful *coup d'état*. The Fatherland Front was a diverse anti-German alliance involving communists, pro-Anglo-American parties and dissatisfied army officers. However, in 1947 it was the communists, supported by the continued presence of the Red Army, who staged a brutal and violent takeover, eventually turning Bulgaria into a People's Republic based on the Soviet model.

After the death of Dimitrov in 1950 there were several leaders before Todor Zhivkov took power in 1954. He was eventually toppled in 1989 by a move initiated from within his own government. However, unlike most other Eastern European countries, the Communist Party in Bulgaria was not immediately banished from the political scene. Instead the 'Bulgarian Communist Party' changed its name to the 'Bulgarian Socialist Party' and won the first free elections in June 1990.

The Bulgarian Socialist Party did not however obtain the two-thirds majority in the Grand National Assembly required in order to alter the Constitution. Unable to consolidate its election victory, the Bulgarian Socialist Party government was forced to resign. A new Constitution was adopted in July 1991 and in October of that year new elections were held. A coalition of non-socialist parties called the Union of Democratic Forces won the largest number of seats but not an overall majority. With the backing of the Movement for Rights and Freedoms (a political party representing Bulgaria's Turkish minority) the Union of Democratic Forces was able to form a workable government under Prime Minister Filip Dimitrov.

In October 1992, Dimitrov resigned as Prime Minister after losing a vote of confidence in the National Assembly. Deputies from the opposition Bulgarian Socialist Party were joined by the Movement for Rights and Freedoms in voting down the Government. It was accused of failing to prevent the collapse of the economy and of selling arms to the former Yugoslavia. In November 1992 (just before this chapter went to press) the Union of Democratic Forces proposed Dimitrov for re-election as Prime Minister.

POLITICAL CHANGE

Having shaken off the shackles of the communist dictatorship, Bulgaria has now emerged as a presidential democracy with a workable legal and constitutional framework within which to live and do business.

The new democratic Constitution which came into force on 13 July 1991 is regarded as being the supreme law of the state and as such no other law may contravene it. Today, power in Bulgaria is shared between the legislature, the executive and the judiciary. Political debate takes place in the National Assembly which consists of 240 members who are elected by a system of proportional representation at least once every four years. It has similar functions to those of the British House of Commons. Matters of constitutional importance are dealt with by the Grand National Assembly – a body of 400 elected members. Decisions regarding the nation's domestic and foreign policy are taken by the Council of Ministers under the leadership and co-ordination of the Prime Minister. The President is responsible for concluding international treaties and promulgating Bulgaria's laws. This post is filled by national elections held every five years.

The restructuring of Bulgaria's economy has gone hand in hand with Bulgaria's transition to democracy; but as has been remarked in Bulgaria, 'a ballot card does not buy a pound of butter'. In essence Bulgaria's economic reform is two-fold. First, the state monopoly on foreign trade has been abolished and Bulgaria's trade is being redirected to a large extent away from the old communist bloc and towards the West. Secondly, a comprehensive privatisation pro-gramme has been formulated. It is hoped that this will attract foreign investment into the country and help to create the market economy which Bulgaria's disciples of capitalism are so impatient to see.

FOREIGN TRADE

Aside from the former Soviet Union, Bulgaria was perhaps affected more than any other Eastern European country by the collapse of communism. The existence of protected and guaranteed markets had led foreign trade to be orientated towards the Soviet Union rather than the West. Indeed, until very recently, 80 per cent of Bulgaria's foreign trade was conducted with the old Soviet bloc, even though it had become increasingly clear by the late 1980s that integration under Comecon had no future.

In the past few years, trade between members of the former Comecon has suffered a sharp decline, if not collapsed altogether. This is partly attributable to the transition to world market prices payable in hard currency as well as reduced deliveries of Soviet oil. Bulgaria has also suffered particularly harshly on account of sanctions imposed by the United Nations on two of its most valuable trading partners – Iraq and Serbia. Consequently, Bulgaria is having to develop new trading relationships and has already forged important links with Greece and Turkey. Furthermore, there is an expectation in Sofia that Bulgaria will sign an assistance agreement with the European Community in 1992.

Bulgaria is also one of the eleven European countries bordering on or in close proximity to the Black Sea. These countries signed a declaration in Istanbul in 1992 creating a 'Black Sea Economic Co-operation Region', although at present this is regarded as more of a gesture of political goodwill rather than the beginnings of a true zone of economic co-operation.

ECONOMIC REFORM

Three years into the reform programme, the economic transformation of Bulgaria is still in its infancy and fraught with uncertainty. It had been hoped that the advent of a new government following the elections of October 1991 and the defeat of the August 1991 'coup' in the Soviet Union would have made the task of those interested in sabotaging the reform of the economic system more difficult. The fall of the government in October 1992 dented this hope. Notwithstanding this setback, there appears to be no turning back on the road to reform.

One of the corner-stones of the reform programme is privatisation. Bulgaria was, however, one of the last Eastern European countries to pass privatisation legislation. The Bill allowing privatisation finally became law in April 1992 and is, in some respects, similar to that of Poland. In particular, there will be no distribution of free shares to the public.

The government's shock therapy was bringing results although the transition to a market economy will undoubtedly be painful and, as in other Eastern European countries, has been accompanied by plunging industrial production, disruption of agriculture and increasing unemployment as central planning and subsidies are eliminated and privatisation proceeds. Since 1989, industrial production has declined by 40 per cent and more than 500,000 workers have become unemployed. Inflation, however, which reached 480 per cent in 1991 sank in the first 8 months of 1992 to an annual rate of 45 per cent, but in August 1992 the increase of retail prices on the previous month was 18 per cent. The exchange rate of the lev against Western currencies has stabilised considerably and Bulgaria is able to boast foreign exchange resources of some US$1.3 billion. Although the country's government debt has been rescheduled by the Paris Club of creditors, agreement has yet to be reached on the private debt with the London Club led by Deutsche Bank.

Bulgaria has attracted only about US$100 million in foreign investment so far (November 1992) and in many cases the level of individual investments is small. Signs of interest by major foreign companies are however increasing. As elsewhere in Eastern Europe, German companies are particularly active and among other sectors tourism, income from which exceeded US$400 million in 1992, is considered to offer particular opportunities.

A new Foreign Investment Law was passed in January 1992. Among other changes, the minimum requirement for investment has been lowered to (at current exchange rates) US$2500, thus opening the door for small-scale investment. Foreign investors are now free to invest in all but a few specified areas which require permits. These are generally areas considered to be sensitive in relation to national security; for example, the acquisition of immovable property in particular geographical areas is restricted. It is thought that this is to stop an economic penetration of south-eastern Bulgaria by Turkish investors.

CONCLUSION

Bulgaria's course since 1989 towards a market economic system has not always been smooth or consistent. The continuing influence of communists in the government was evident until recently in most debates on important items of legislation; it should be remembered that Todor Zhivkov was deposed in November 1989 not by a popular revolution but by a 'palace coup'. The Lukanov government which replaced Zhivkov pursued a very cautious line throughout 1990 and, even after the elections of June 1990 in which the socialists obtained a majority, the government was barely able to maintain the political stability necessary to pursue a consistent legislative course. Since January 1991, however, the pace of reform has quickened dramatically and, despite the recent hiccough, it seems that Bulgaria is committed to a consistent programme of economic reform.

2

Economic Reform

SG Warburg

FORMER ECONOMIC STRUCTURE

While Bulgaria's economy at the end of World War II was primarily based on agriculture, with a relatively small industrial sector, over the next two decades it was transformed by the new communist government into one in which industry was predominant. A strong centralised planning system was established, giving priority to expanding production in the nationalised industrial sector. High rates of economic growth were achieved, which averaged, according to official statistics, 7 to 8 per cent per annum. However, the increase in output was only achieved at the expense of efficiency and quality, and the consumer goods and agricultural sectors in particular were given insufficient regard.

In the 1970s and 1980s a number of structural economic problems emerged. The pace of technological change slowed down. An artificial system of subsidies and prices resulted in misallocation of resources and environmental pollution. The shielding of the Bulgarian economy from international competition, due to strong trade links with Comecon countries, increased the inefficiency of industry. While the strong ties with Comecon provided a market for manufacturing sector exports, it also made Bulgaria increasingly vulnerable to economic developments in Comecon countries, and in the USSR in particular. During the 1980s, economic growth and investment slowed significantly and a persistent balance of payments deficit with Western countries emerged. To finance this deficit, foreign currency debt, predominantly to commercial banks, grew from around US$3 billion in 1985 to over US$12 billion in 1992.

With the dissolution of Comecon in 1990, the economic situation deteriorated markedly in Bulgaria. On the one hand, export markets disappeared while, on the other hand, scarcities in essential raw materials and energy supplies emerged. An additional external shock was provided by the Middle East crisis, which had a particularly strong impact on Bulgaria due to its dependence on trade with Iraq. As a result, the trade balance recorded a US$785 million deficit at the end of 1990, reserves dropped to around US$200 million, while the debt moratorium declared in March 1990 shut the country off from access to foreign credits. The result was a drastic fall in imports and a consequent fall in production, with a 10 per cent decline in GDP in 1990.

THE REFORM PACKAGE

The IMF-endorsed economic reform programme, which the country embarked on February 1991, is an attempt to tackle the serious domestic and external problems which had emerged. A major feature was the comparative degree of political consensus for reform, which ensured that the process was embarked on swiftly.

Having joined the World Bank and the IMF in September 1990, Bulgaria implemented (beginning in February 1991) a wide-ranging programme of liberalisation and reform. A stand-by arrangement, concluded in March 1991, triggered a SDR279 million facility, the disbursement of which was conditional on the implementation of a number of specific measures. The main elements of Bulgaria's reform programme included:

1. *Monetary policy:* interest rates were increased and credit conditions were tightened.

2. *Income policy:* wages came under strict control in order to thwart hyperinflation.

3. *Price liberalisation:* almost all administered prices were abolished with the exception of electricity, heating and essential foodstuffs.

4. *Exchange rate reform:* following earlier attempts at reform in 1990, a unified floating exchange rate was introduced in February 1991, based on an inter-bank foreign exchange market.

5. *Competition and privatisation:* a review of public sector firms was initiated, which concentrated on demonopolisation and introduction of commercial practices. The government enacted a new Commercial Law, a Privatisation Law, a law on the

Table 2.1   *Output, prices and the labour market, 1990–91*

	1990	*1991*
Gross domestic product		
At current prices (Lev billion)	45.4	130.0
At 1990 prices (Lev billion)	45.4	35.0
GDP deflator (% change)	23.8%	271.4%
Exchange rate (Lev/US$, end of year)	2.75	18.1
Retail price index (year-on-year change)	26.3%	479.8%
Average monthly wage in Lev	361	887
Real change, retail prices	7.8%	– 57.6%
Employment (public sector, thousands)	3846	3204
Unemployment		
Thousands, end of year	65	419
In % of labour force	1.6%	10.5%

Source: National Statistical Institute.

organisation of the central and commercial banks, and a Foreign Investment Law. Following passage of the Privatisation Law in April 1992, the government embarked on an ambitious sectoral privatisation programme sponsored by the PHARE programme.

6. *Foreign trade policy:* import and export quotas were virtually abolished, as were subsidies to exports. At the same time, enterprises were allowed to trade directly with any foreign enterprise.

7. *Foreign debt:* following Bulgaria's debt moratorium in March 1990, negotiations commenced with Bulgaria's official and commercial bank creditors to restructure the country's external liabilities.

ECONOMIC PERFORMANCE

Despite the economic weaknesses described above, and Bulgaria's great vulnerability to external shocks, the country has made substantial progress in the implementation of its reform programme.

These results were achieved despite a deteriorating external environment throughout 1991. Inflows of funds from the West did not meet the level promised by the group of 24 developed industrial nations (G-24) after the conclusion of the stand-by arrangement with

Table 2.2 *Balance of payments, 1990–91 (US$ billion)*

	1990	*1991*
Current account balance	−1.3	−0.9
Trade balance	−0.8	0.0
Exports	2.6	3.4
Imports	3.4	3.4
Services and transfers, net	−0.5	−0.9
O/W interest due	0.8	0.9
Other capital[1]	−2.2	−1.2
Reserves change (increase = −)	0.9	−0.6
Change in arrears	0.4	−0.4
Financing requirement	2.2	3.1
Financing	2.2	3.1
Private capital	2.2	1.5
Direct investment	–	–
Debt relief	2.2	1.5
Official capital	–	1.6
IMF[2]	–	0.4
World Bank	–	0.1
EIB/EBRD	–	–
G-24[3]	–	0.2
Debt relief	–	0.9

[1] Includes scheduled amortisation and short-term credits.
[2] Disbursements from the IMF during 1991 were lower than originally expected by SDR32.6 million (about US$45 million at current exchange rates). Bulgaria did not qualify for a second drawing under the Compensatory Financing Facility because of lower than expected imports of energy products.
[3] Of the US$800 million requested, G-24 pledged US$600 million and disbursed US$200 million (first tranche of EC contribution) during 1991. The remainder (US$400 million) was expected to have been largely disbursed by the end of 1992.

Source: National Bank of Bulgaria.

the IMF. As a result, imports continued their sharp decline for the first part of the year, thereby exacerbating the fall in output and GDP. However, trade with the rest of the world picked up during the second half of the year as the earlier devaluation stimulated exports of a wide range of products. The recovery in trade, together with a strict foreign exchange policy and the debt moratorium, were the main factors behind the rise in gross official foreign exchange reserves by US$0.6 billion during the period.

During 1991 most economic variables indicate that a severe adjustment effort took place initially, followed by an improvement in the second half of the year. Real GDP is estimated to have declined by 23 per cent in 1991. All sectors of the economy were affected, particularly industrial activity, but also agriculture and services. Inflation overshot significantly in the wake of the price liberalisation and foreign exchange reform. After rising by more than 170 per cent in February and March 1991, largely as a result of the massive devaluation of the lev, retail price inflation was, on average, less than 5 per cent monthly during the remainder of the year. Employment was hit by layoffs in the public sector, and real wages declined steeply.

Against this background, Bulgaria has continued to press ahead with its programme of structural reform. In mid-1991, a Foreign Investment Law was passed which was revised in January 1992 in order to provide an even more liberal framework for foreign business. In April 1992, a Privatisation Law was adopted which contained substantial incentives to private investment including a provision for the use of debt for equity swaps. It is too early to say whether the reform process has been successful, since the effects of the adjustment process are still being felt. Encouragingly, however, the commitment to reform remains strong along with the realisation that there are no real alternatives.

EXTERNAL DEBT

Bulgaria's fundamental problem is the very high level of external indebtedness which, at the end of 1992, was over US$12 billion. The two principal features of its debt are that (i) over 80 per cent is owed to commercial banks and (ii) a large part is short term. The debt crisis was triggered in early 1990 by the lack of convertible currency which coincided with a heavy bunching of scheduled foreign debt service payments. The government announced a moratorium on principal payments on 29 March 1990. Subsequent negotiations with the commercial banks led to an extension of the moratorium on principal and the suspension of interest payments until the end of 1990. At the same time, new commercial bank credits as well as trade lines ended.

Negotiations with creditors concentrated on how to approach a comprehensive restructuring of Bulgaria's debt. In May 1991, the new administration reached agreement with the Paris Club on a rescheduling of Bulgaria's official debt over 10 years, with six years' grace. A similar comprehensive agreement has yet to be reached with the commercial banks which have up until now continued to grant

Table 2.3   *Bulgaria's external debt, 1985–90 (US$ million)*

	1985	1986	1987	1988	1989	1990	1991
Total debt	3,994	5,244	7,072	9,128	10,213	10,927	11,923
Long-term debt	3,944	5,184	6,721	8,499	9,359	9,564	11,023
Public and publicly guaranteed	3,944	5,184	6,721	8,499	9,359	9,564	11,023
Official creditors	443	504	505	617	643	664	2,612
Multilateral	420	471	432	521	539	552	549
Concessional	0	0	0	0	0	0	0
IDA	0	0	0	0	0	0	0
Non-concessional	420	471	432	521	539	552	549
IBRD	0	0	0	0	0	0	61
Bilateral	23	33	73	96	104	112	2,063
Concessional	0	0	0	0	0	0	0
Private creditors	3,521	4,700	6,232	7,882	8,716	8,900	8,411
Bonds	0	0	0	0	257	283	292
Commercial banks	1,959	2,113	2,656	3,193	3,421	3,538	5,242
Other private	1,562	2,587	3,576	4,689	5,038	5,079	2,877
Private non-guaranteed	0	0	0	0	0	0	0
Debt outstanding long term	3,944	5,184	6,721	8,499	9,359	9,564	11,023
Short-term debt	50	60	351	629	854	1,363	487

Source: World Bank, World Debt Tables.

Bulgaria successive three-month roll overs of maturities of principal and interest, while a more permanent solution is negotiated.

In April 1992, discussions started between Bulgaria and the consultative committee of the London Club on a debt reduction package. The proposals tabled by Bulgaria included provision for a debt buy-back and conversion programme. Substantive negotiations have begun, but an agreement has yet to emerge.

OUTLOOK

In April 1992 the government's economic programme was boosted by the approval by the IMF of a US$212 million stand-by credit for a further 12 months. This credit came as an endorsement of the government's strict austerity budget, in which among other objectives a budget deficit target of 4.3 per cent of GDP was set. Despite some uncertainty as to Bulgaria's chances of meeting these targets, further support is expected from the West. The World Bank, the G–24, the European Community, the EBRD and the OECD have indicated their willingness to support the economic reform programme. After officials from the IMF were reported to have been favourably impressed by the course of the reform programme, it is possible that Bulgaria may receive a three-year extended fund facility in early 1993.

Bulgaria's most serious problem remains the unsustainable level of debt stock and its consequential debt service obligations. In June 1992 the debt to GDP ratio was estimated at 150 per cent and the debt to exports ratio at 270 per cent. In this situation, agreement on a comprehensive debt package has become fundamental to maintaining the pace of economic reform, securing a resumption of capital inflows, and ensuring a lasting solution to Bulgaria's external problems. If a reduction in debt stock and service could be achieved along the lines of the Brady Plan (possibly with enhancements provided under the auspices of an extended fund facility) it is likely that the pace of economic reforms would pick up with consequential improvements in performance.

3

Market Potential

Cerrex Ltd

This chapter provides a background to Bulgaria, its resources, expected priority areas and present trade patterns with the UK. It should be looked at jointly with Appendix 1 which elaborates on the prospects referred to briefly in this chapter, and examines in more depth some 20 economic sectors.

NATURAL FEATURES

Bulgaria occupies a strategic position in the centre of the Balkan peninsular, being the natural route for goods and services traded between Europe and the Middle East and North Africa. It has common borders with Turkey and Greece in the south, the former Yugoslavia in the west and Romania in the north. To the east is the Black Sea with a coastline of 233 miles. The country has a length of some 323 miles and a width of 205 miles and is just under half the total area of the UK.

The climate is mainly continental, with hot dry summers and cold winters. In the north of the country lies the Danube Plain, while the centre of the country is dominated by the Balkan Mountains and the fertile Central Plain. In the south, facing the Greek border, are the Rhodope Mountains which reach nearly 10,000 feet. This is an area of great natural beauty and is expected to continue to develop as a tourist centre.

The population of nearly 9 million makes it the smallest country (except for Albania) of the former centrally planned Eastern European economies. Population growth over the past 10 years has been minimal – recent figures record a small decline. Some 6 million Bulgarians are urban dwellers (67 per cent compared with 62 per

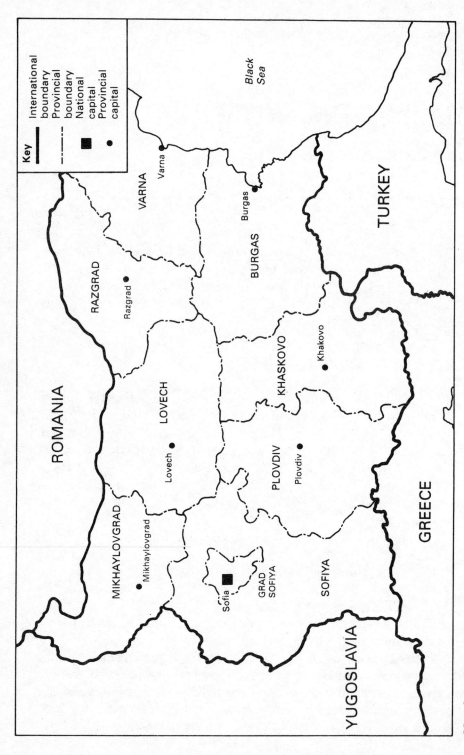

Map 3.1 *Bulgaria and its neighbours*

cent 10 years ago), which reflects the lack of emphasis in past development plans on the agricultural sector.

The population is relatively homogeneous (over 90 per cent Bulgar) and suffers less from minority and ethnic problems which beset many other Eastern European countries. The official language is Bulgarian written in cyrillic script, although some Turkish is spoken. Traditionally, the most common second languages were Russian, German and French, although English is becoming more widely understood. The per capita GNP of Bulgaria is US$3690, a little less than Hungary and Poland but nearly twice that of Romania.

The capital Sofia, with a population of 1,141,000, is situated on the River Iskar in a fertile mountain basin. It is not only the centre for political, economic and cultural activities but is a major industrial area, particularly for engineering. Other important cities are Plovdiv (population 360,000 and a centre for engineering and electronics); the port of Varna (300,000 – engineering, food processing and chemicals); Rousse (178,000 – engineering, leather and shipbuilding); the port of Bourgas (metalworking and petrochemicals); Stara Zagora (electronics, textiles and fertilisers); and Pleven (food processing, textiles and petrochemicals).

TRANSPORT INFRASTRUCTURE

A widespread railway system connects Sofia with neighbouring countries and with the coast. Most of the railway equipment and locomotives were bought from the USSR as Bulgaria has little capacity in this field. International transport of goods is provided not only by rail but by a very large international road haulage system.

There is a small merchant fleet, using the Black Sea and to a lesser extent the Danube, which carries both domestic and international traffic. Varna and Bourgas are the only sea ports of any significance and because of their location have developed as industrial centres.

RAW MATERIALS

Bulgaria has relatively few natural resources except for fertile soil, large reserves of low quality coal and large areas of forest (both broad leaved and coniferous) covering about one-third of the country. There are limited deposits of iron ore, uranium, lead, zinc, wolfram and copper, together with very small deposits of gold and silver.

INDUSTRY

Bulgarian industry employs 1.5 million people and accounts for 67 per cent of gross material product and 57 per cent of national income.

Privatisation has started, although industry is still largely state owned. At the time of writing, some 10 per cent of Bulgaria's industry has been privatised. Capital goods represent two-thirds of production and consumer goods one-third, proportions which have remained the same over the past 10 years in spite of efforts to increase the supply of consumer goods to the Bulgarian market.

SOME MAJOR OPPORTUNITIES

Since 1990, Bulgaria has faced a period of considerable upheaval. During 1991, against a background of default on payment of debts and interest, production fell by about 20 per cent, massive inflation

Table 3.1   *Share of total industrial production (in % at constant prices)**

Sector	1980	1989	1990	1991
Capital goods	65.9	65.7	65.5	–
Consumer goods	34.1	34.3	34.5	–
Electricity	4.0	3.6	4.9	6.3
Coal mining	1.5	1.3	1.3	1.4
Oil and gas	0.3	–	–	–
Ferrous metallurgy	4.2	3.0	3.3	2.7
Non-ferrous metallurgy	3.1	2.3	2.4	2.3
Electrical machinery	23.8	34.6	31.0	25.4
Metalworking machines	15.6	17.9	17.7	16.0
Electronics	8.2	16.7	13.3	9.4
Chemicals, plastics and rubber	18.1	15.2	12.6	12.3
Building materials	3.6	2.4	2.5	2.3
Wood and wood products	3.4	2.7	2.8	2.8
Glass and china earthenware	1.1	0.8	1.0	1.1
Paper and paper products	1.6	1.1	1.1	1.2
Textiles and knitwear	5.4	5.3	6.0	5.8
Ready-made clothing	1.8	2.1	2.7	2.7
Leather, fur and footwear	1.3	1.4	1.6	1.8
Printing and publishing	0.6	0.4	0.6	0.9
Food products	22.1	20.5	22.9	27.8
Other	4.1	3.3	3.3	3.2

Source: *Statistical Reference Book of the Republic of Bulgaria, 1991 and 1992.*

* Percentages do not add up to 100 per cent as there is some double counting.

took place and unemployment rose to over 10 per cent. Trade declined to almost all markets – most of all to the country's traditional Comecon markets where the decline averaged over 80 per cent.

The picture is now brighter than it was two years ago. Bulgaria has improved political links with the West and recent efforts to move towards a market economy have earned praise from the IMF among others. Inflation has fallen from the very high levels of 1990. Export earnings have held up well, there is greater political stability and a solid base of support has arisen for government policies. Much of the press, including the newly established daily paper *Continent*, is urging the government to accelerate privatisation and give greater encouragement to joint ventures. Even among the opposition there appears to be an acceptance of the need to move towards a free market economy. With the passage of the 1992 Privatisation Law, the country has made clear its support for reform, privatisation and foreign investment, while the Bulgarian government is keen to develop joint venture companies and deals that bring in investment and modernisation.

Nonetheless, 1992 was a difficult and very important year. Some

Table 3.2   *Employment in industry ('000)*

Sector	1980	1989	1990	1991
Electricity	25	36	38	37
Coal mining	43	47	44	43
Oil and gas	0.5	0.5	0.5	0.5
Ferrous metallurgy	34	39	29	24
Non-ferrous metallurgy	37	43	46	40
Electrical machinery	365	558	517	398
Metalworking machinery	239	345	319	245
Electronics	126	213	198	153
Chemicals, plastics and rubber	97	113	111	95
Building materials	63	58	51	41
Wood and wood products	73	69	65	55
Paper and paper products	18	19	18	16
Glass and china earthenware	26	24	23	20
Textiles and knitwear	128	118	113	89
Ready-made clothes	64	80	84	66
Leather, fur and footwear	29	35	33	27
Printing and publishing	11	10	9	7
Food products	172	177	168	143
Other	163	144	123	85

Source: *Statistical Reference Book of the Republic of Bulgaria, 1991 and 1992.*

major industries such as engineering and electronics have been among the sectors facing greatest difficulties as a result of the change towards a market economy, and the country can no longer rely on exporting over 80 per cent of its output to Comecon countries against minimal international competition. Many of Bulgaria's products are not competitive in Western Europe and resources available will need to go into expanding the export sector, modernisation of plant and improvements in marketing and training in order to rectify this problem.

Although the Agency for Privatisation has been established, its role has not yet been clarified and privatisation plans for most of the sectors have yet to be developed. Also, there remains a large debt to service. The country is behind Czechoslovakia, Poland and Hungary in its development towards a market economy and, although this might allow it to avoid some of the mistakes made by other countries, it has been placed at an initial disadvantage in obtaining access to the limited funds available to firms considering investment in Eastern Europe. Its geographical location makes it a fine centre for those companies wishing to use it as a bridge to trade in new markets in the Middle East, North Africa and parts of the former USSR, but makes it more distant from most Western European markets. It has traditionally been more isolated from Western business methods than most other countries of Eastern Europe, although the development of wine production and light industry has shown that it can produce quality products and successfully market them.

Like all previously centrally planned economies, Bulgaria has a shortage of domestically generated funds and very limited money is available for direct purchases from the West. All Eastern European countries have seen an initial rush towards the purchase of consumer products, but those seeking to sell consumer goods must bear in mind that local wage levels (average monthly salaries of those in employment are estimated at about £60) will make it difficult to sustain a market. There will be strong competition from sources such as Greece and Turkey – the latter is the only market of note to have increased its bilateral trade with Bulgaria during 1991. The external debt moratorium imposed two years ago by the Bulgarians has also affected the availability of credit as well as damaging confidence.

Sectoral analysis

Initial opportunities will be in those sectors where aid funds are available and in investment and co-operation. PHARE, World Bank,

EBRD and other programmes are aimed at priority areas – energy/environment, industrial restructuring (including chemicals and light industries), investment in transport and telecommunications, health, agriculture and agricultural processing and technical assistance/consultancy know-how.

Major opportunities will also come in those areas where there has been a tradition of sales to hard currency markets or access to foreign exchange. These include some of those which benefit from aid but also services in general – tourism, wine, infrastructure, some parts of light industry and distribution.

In agriculture and tourism, Bulgaria has the potential to compete internationally without substantial extra investment. These are areas where the country has had some experience of the market economy, both sectors being labour intensive and having the potential to counteract rising unemployment.

With fertile soil and a good climate, Bulgaria has always had large agricultural and food processing industries, although they have been somewhat neglected in the past 20 years. It has been losing market share in the former Eastern bloc countries and, during the past year, there have been some surpluses for export to the West of a number of products. The farming sector will require to be restructured, modern food processing and packaging machinery to be installed, modern management put in place, and decisive action taken to encourage people back to the land. The wine industry has already been successful in Western Europe, but still needs investment in, for example, new vineyards – which will take four to five years before they become fully productive – and modern processing machinery. The tobacco and cigarette industries are expected to make a similar export effort.

Tourism has less strong traditions. For much of the past 25 years, it has been targeted at large package groups from Eastern Europe (mainly to the Black Sea resorts) and it has proved difficult to attract richer Western tourists. The potential however is enormous and the sector is an investment priority. The country can appeal to tourists all the year round, with skiing facilities in the winter, beach holidays on the Black Sea in the summer, together with historic and cultural towns. Tourists from the Eastern bloc were not large spenders and were satisfied with self-catering, cheaper quality hotels and fewer restaurants, amusement and sport facilities. Bulgaria will need to attract big hotel chains, appeal to the family holiday maker, and to upgrade hotels, their equipment, management and ancillary services.

If it is to be successful in encouraging tourists and business,

Bulgaria will also need to upgrade transport and infrastructure. Full integration into the European road networks, modernisation of major airports at Sofia, Varna, Plovdiv and Bourgas, the possible construction of more international airports, agreement on air traffic and landing rights, and the improvement of telecommunications systems will all need priority attention.

Industrial modernisation

Industry presents a more complicated picture. Domestic demand is small so a major effort will need to be made to achieve sales to non-Comecon countries. Light industry is expected to continue to decline initially – there was a drop in output of about 10 per cent in 1991, due mainly to the loss of major markets – but the country has strong traditions in clothing and knitwear, ready-made suits, furniture, glass, leather and footwear, all of which have established considerable export markets. These are all industries which Bulgaria sees as priorities for modernisation and development and are obvious areas for joint ventures and co-operation.

By Western standards a substantial part of heavy industry is outdated and uncompetitive in world markets. Many sectors are labour and energy intensive and environmentally poor, but this is by no means true throughout. Bulgaria made substantial investments in computers, electronics and robotics for numerically controlled metal cutting machines (where it developed as the centre for Comecon as a whole). Such high-tec industries and parts of heavy engineering are already in discussions with Western companies in an effort to find additional suitable joint venture partners. Over the longer term, present price advantages will be reduced and unless there is a clear policy that successfully encourages modernisation and inward investment, whole sectors of heavy industry could decline.

Energy shortages and misuse are a major constraint on the Bulgarian economy. Initial emphasis will have to be directed towards alternative sources of energy, energy saving and moving the cost of energy on to a more commercial basis. Environmental concerns over Kozlodui and the shortage of domestically produced power means that a large proportion of Bulgaria's resources will need to be spent initially on generating safe and cheap alternative power for industry and consumers, and, at first, this will probably be the main area for international aid.

Funds available through PHARE, KHF (Know-How Fund), JICAP (British Council) and others are aimed at bringing about a transfer of management know-how and other skills, as well as part funding the services required to develop the infrastructure for a market economy. This would include, for example, financial services (management consultancy, accountancy and banking, where a major need will be to help in the privatisation process and establish sector programmes), marketing expertise and engineering skills. General service industries such as dry cleaners, supermarkets and restaurants are also areas in need of development.

UK TRADE WITH BULGARIA

Bulgaria ran a positive balance of payments with most Western countries in the early-1980s, but exports in hard currency stagnated during the latter part of the decade. This reflected the steady deterioration in the competitiveness of Bulgarian manufacturing industry, the declining value and volume of oil exports, and debts incurred in sales to certain developing countries. In 1989, Bulgaria's major exports were machinery and equipment, fuel, minerals and metals, followed by processed foodstuffs, raw materials, consumer goods (including clothing, sports accessories, furniture, carpets, ceramics and electronic products) and agricultural goods and chemicals. Imports from the West comprised about 40 per cent machinery and transport equipment (especially specialised machin-

Table 3.3 *Major UK exports to Bulgaria, 1990–92 (by value – £'000)*

	1990	1991	Jan–Sept 1991	1992
Total exports of which:	**45,022**	**35,647**	**24,909**	**37,706**
1. Beverages	3,767	3,809	2,120	7,248
2. Textile fibres	2,897	1,767	1,527	2,347
3. General industrial equipment	4,537	2,389	1,766	2,318
4. Road vehicles	949	810	768	2,242
5. Medicines and pharmaceuticals	517	2,217	1,053	2,180
6. Chemical materials	3,277	1,934	1,776	2,153
7. Office equipment and ADP equipment	1,741	1,630	779	2,018
8. Power generating machinery	1,833	2,180	951	1,457
9. Professional and scientific equipment	1,451	1,013	652	1,434
10. Miscellaneous manufactured items	1,642	2,013	1,597	1,154

Source: Department of Trade and Industry.

Table 3.4   *Major UK imports from Bulgaria, 1990–92 (by value – £'000)*

	1990	1991	Jan–Sept 1991	1992
Total imports	**32,787**	**36,786**	**20,609**	**34,636**
of which:				
1. Beverages	11,729	13,288	9,975	9,266
2. Apparel and clothing	1,461	2,964	1,470	5,041
3. Footwear	425	1,275	790	3,124
4. Miscellaneous manufactured articles	858	1,571	83	2,198
5. Metal ores and scrap	121	541	318	2,187
6. Non-ferrous metals	18	176	21	1,503
7. Textile yarn and fabrics	179	568	449	1,274
8. Manufactured fertilisers	3,893	3,503	2,448	1,179
9. Non-metallic minerals	454	1,083	954	728
10. General industrial machinery	3,906	948	653	706

Source: Department of Trade and Industry.

ery for textiles, food, chemicals and paper), followed by food processing and packaging, food, beverages and tobacco.

Until the beginning of 1990, Bulgaria had a substantial negative balance of payments with the UK and on a per capita basis, UK exports to Bulgaria exceeded those (for example) to Czechoslovakia. At the end of 1990, however, UK exports fell sharply as a result of shortages of hard currency and lack of confidence in Bulgaria's financial position. This substantially reduced the country's trade deficit with the UK.

Bulgaria's recent ability to pay for imports has however been underpinned by funds from the World Bank, Japan's EXIM Bank and the IMF. The country made proposals for rescheduling commercial debts to creditor banks in April 1992, having stalled since March 1990, and financial confidence has been increasing. In the middle of 1992, the country made its first payment on interest on debt for over two years and the government is reporting greater optimism over negotiations on foreign commercial debts. The exchange rate has shown greater stability than most other countries within Eastern Europe and inflation has come down. Trade figures in dollar terms show a continuing export growth and imports from OECD countries have replaced many of those from the former CMEA countries. Bulgaria has re-established some of its former markets in the Middle East, North Africa and Eastern Europe. On present indications, funds available from direct exports by the Bulgarians during 1992 and 1993 are expected to be below their 1989 level, but above that of 1991.

UK trade with Bulgaria is expected to expand by up to 50 per cent in value terms for the year 1992 compared to 1991. Whether this will be maintained into 1993 will depend on the continuing confidence of the banks, the maintenance of political stability and a favourable outcome of the EC negotiations with Bulgaria primarily in the areas of steel, textiles and agriculture. An added impetus to UK–Bulgaria trade will be the setting up of a UK–Bulgaria Chamber of Commerce in London, planned for early 1993.

Among the UK's traditional major exports to Bulgaria are power generation, iron and steel, electronic kits for assembly, beverages (not all, however, for local consumption), supplies for the glass industry, fertilisers, clothing, office machinery, medical and pharmaceutical products and telecommunications equipment. UK companies involved in such trade have included a large variety of beverage and whisky companies, Rank Xerox, ICL, Plessey, ICI, Courtaulds, Perkins, Glaxo and APV; these companies are all in sectors where a long-term expansion of trade seems likely. Increased sales in the environment and energy sectors, power generation equipment, consumer goods, telecommunications equipment, machine tools and other requirements for modernising industry, and the hotel and tourist infrastructure are also to be expected.

UK imports have been dominated by imports of wine (one-third of total shipments in 1991). Wine has been well marketed in the UK and, as long as the problems of the wine growing industry do not undermine exports of the product, it is expected to continue as one of the success stories of the Bulgarian export effort.

Wine sales could open the way for increased future sales of food and processed foodstuffs. When the present difficulties Bulgaria is facing in the agricultural sector are resolved, the country will be expected to have a surplus of a number of such agricultural products for export and, given the right marketing, packaging and quality control, these could find a good market in the UK and elsewhere in Europe. Other products where it is possible to see increased exports to the UK include textiles, footwear, electronic products, light industry generally, and sub-component manufacture – the potential for other sales to the UK will depend heavily on Bulgaria being able to restructure and offer competitive products required in the West.

4

Business Culture

Touche Ross

Under socialism, Bulgarian economic policy was pursued through the system of central planning and centralised allocation of investments. Its priorities were industrialisation, concentration and specialisation of production capacities, and technological and structural changes (based on integration with the USSR and Comecon). The state had a monopoly on overall economic activity – almost 100 per cent of the productive capital stock in industry being state owned. The monopoly rights of the state extended to foreign economic relations, banking and lending, and foreign exchange transactions.

The Central Planning Committee decided upon the level and pricing of inputs and outputs for all enterprises, as well as upon their relationships with business partners, etc. As a result of this concentration of production, there emerged about 20 huge industrial conglomerates with highly diversified activities including production operations, research and development, design, construction, engineering, marketing, consulting, export and import transactions, retail trade and services.

Big conglomerates, organised in a highly monopolistic fashion, were preferred because integrating them into the overall plan was considerably easier than dealing with smaller firms. Protection against foreign competition, as well as the impossibility of bankruptcy, further reduced the incentives for efficient production. Subsidies compensated for state enterprises' financial losses either directly from the budget or indirectly through the banking system and domestic price mechanism. Price levels were set in an administrative way that failed to take account of market forces and economic considerations.

Managers of state-owned enterprises were appointed by the Council of Ministers, the relevant ministries and other government agencies. When selecting executive staff, managerial competency, training and skills were taken into account, although political loyalty was regarded as the main selection criterion. Central planning meant managers had limited opportunity for strategic decision making or to implement their managerial concepts. The complicated organisational structures and communications within the enterprises eliminated personal responsibility. The plan, along with the lack of economic motivation for personnel (both management and production), discouraged risk taking and personal initiative.

In the 1980s, certain changes in the system of central planning were introduced: the number of mandatory 'planning indicators' was gradually diminished and the quantitative (unit) indicators were replaced by value ones.

With the liberalisation of economic activities and the abolition of state monopolies, Bulgarian enterprises are undergoing substantial transformation and restructuring. At present, old and new institutions are operating in parallel, the former already discredited and with decreasing effectiveness. The following new trends should be underlined:

■ The first steps are being taken towards decentralisation of economic decision making, including the extension of foreign trade rights of individual proprietors, private and co-operative firms.

■ Involvement of private entrepreneurs or middlemen in operations, domestic trade and foreign trade activities.

■ Fostering competition by cutting subsidies and establishing a commercial basis for access to credits.

■ Installing an incentive system designed to make managers more concerned about ecology, profitability and the value of assets under their control.

These new trends may indicate a gradual change in managerial attitudes in the existing state sector as well as in the emerging private one.

The new legal framework for fundamental change in the structure of Bulgarian enterprises was introduced by the Trade Act in July 1991. The Act provides a unified legal and regulatory basis for conducting both private and public sector business, including provision for the transformation of state organisations into public companies.

STATE ENTERPRISES

The state-owned enterprise is still the predominant form of business organisation in Bulgaria. State companies play a crucial role in all sectors of the national economy and their assets account for about 95 per cent of the country's total capital stocks.

State-owned enterprises are of two basic legal types. There are the state business enterprises (state companies or firms), and state enterprises which do not constitute companies (state corporations).

State firms today are self-managed business entities. They determine their internal organisational and production structure, their rights, obligations and responsibilities as well as their management. The management bodies of a state firm include the general assembly of personnel, the board of management, the board of comptrollers and the executive director. The general assembly of personnel examines the company's plan and votes on guidelines for the social development of personnel. The board of management is responsible for the day-to-day operations of the firm and can decide upon adoption of the company's constitution; election and dismissal of the chairman of the board, the executive director and his deputies; approval of the annual report and the annual balance sheet; aims and objectives; strategic planning, and approval of development projects; pay scales and financial incentives for officials it has elected; establishment or liquidation of affiliates and subsidiaries; and issuing of bonds and shares.

State-owned companies have been free since April 1989 to conduct foreign trade alone or via foreign trade organisations, trade representatives, agents and intermediaries. The foreign exchange regulations (Ordinance 15 of February 1991) permit state firms to retain foreign currency obtained from the export of goods and services, as well as foreign currency credits granted by Bulgarian and foreign banks, in special accounts kept with the various Bulgarian commercial banks. They are also allowed to purchase freely foreign currency from the commercial banks and other institutions authorised to operate on the local foreign exchange market. Recent amendments to Ordinance 15 also allow inter-company trade in foreign exchange receipts.

State-owned enterprises are undergoing significant changes with the privatisation and reform of public enterprises, the first steps being demonopolisation and the breaking up of large economic structures into smaller units. Public enterprise reform must generally precede privatisation because before being privatised state-owned companies are restructured or consolidated. In certain cases, closures cannot be avoided.

Commercialisation is taking place in compliance with the provisions of the Trade Act. Under the Act, state enterprises are subject to incorporation or are transformed into new classes of companies, the most usual being the sole proprietor limited liability company and the sole proprietor joint stock company ('sole proprietor' indicating that the state is the sole owner of the assets). The Council of Ministers determines the statutory capital, approves the constitution of the joint stock or limited liability company and appoints a provisional board, board of comptrollers and executive director. It also determines the number of shares for sale and the conditions of the sale. The joint stock company takes over all assets and liabilities and other rights and obligations of the transformed state firm.

A government institution, the Agency for Privatisation, has been created in order to represent the state as an owner and to assist with the transformation of state-owned entities.

Bulgaria is considered a 'late starter' in business restructuring. Many political, economic and social questions need to be taken into account, not least because political power was only lost by the former Communist Party in October 1991. Recent public opinion polls suggest that Bulgarian society is still not prepared to accept an unequal distribution of wealth and regards private property as the main cause of inequality. The breaking up of monopolistic structures has until now been ineffective and steps made so far must be reconsidered. Many companies are not viable because they cannot be restructured or have bad debts or obsolete productive stocks. The domestic capital market is not yet functioning and savings are rather limited relative to the value of the assets which are to be sold.

Since the business environment in Bulgaria is still not market-oriented and state enterprises are in a period of transition, managers are required to act in hostile external and internal economic conditions and in a very dynamic legal environment. They are expected to devise and implement viable solutions with scarce resources and, in many cases, management decisions are taken under political or trade union pressure.

During incorporation and commercialisation, state-owned enterprises maintain direct contact with the Council of Ministers and other government agencies. However, when these stages are completed, they are independent business entities, although they remain subject to indirect methods of management and control (for example, through the banking and financial system, taxation, interest rates and exchange rate policies). State orders for production and deliveries are handled on a commercial basis.

It is expected that more than 2000 new state firms will be registered in 1992. Until now only about 700 state firms have been established, predominantly in the field of food and beverage industries. There are a few new projects in the metallurgy, engineering and electronics fields. Progress has been particularly slow as regards transport, communications, pharmaceuticals, tourism and other services.

CO-OPERATIVES

Co-operatives are quite widespread in Bulgaria. Prior to the collectivisation of the land, co-operatives were the predominant business form in the sectors of agriculture, wine production, retailing, banking and insurance. Since the enactment of the Restitution Act many of the former co-operatives have been restored and are now resuming their traditional activities. Their establishment and activities are now regulated by the Law on Co-operatives, in force since August 1991.

Co-operatives can be organised in all spheres of economic activity. Five main types of co-operative enterprises can be distinguished, namely:

1. Consumers' co-operatives. These cover trade, catering, tourism, confectionery, foods and beverages, processing of fruits and vegetables, public utilities, etc. They are most popular in the agricultural parts of the country.

2. Producers' co-operatives. They engage in various types of economic activities such as services and the production of a limited range of consumer goods manufactured for sale on the domestic market and for export. These co-operatives are typically located in cities and towns.

3. Pupils' and undergraduate students' co-operatives. They have a lot in common with producers' co-operatives, enjoying at the same time tax reliefs and customs duty exemptions.

4. Producers' co-operatives of the disabled.

5. Agricultural co-operatives (co-operative farms). These engage in

all types of agricultural production, mainly grain production and cattle breeding. According to the newly accepted regulations on land ownership and restitution, the existing co-operatives and state farms are to be liquidated. After the restoration of property rights the new (in fact, the previous) private owners will be free to dispose of the land. Recent polls indicate that 41 per cent of the arable land will be subject to privatisation and 2 million landowners will emerge. From these, 15 per cent intend to set up family farms, 75 per cent to enter into newly formed co-operative associations, and 10 per cent to sell or lease their land.

Generally, co-operative associations are recognised as being dominant in the sphere of agriculture. They are also expected to play a substantial role in banking and lending, supply and distribution, services and foreign trade, in part because of tax incentives offered to certain types of co-operatives such as those organised by students and the disabled. In fact, banking and insurance may only be carried out by a joint stock company or a co-operative enterprise; the latter has the advantage of requiring no minimum authorised capital while the absence of a stock exchange and delay in privatisation of state enterprises has adversely influenced the former.

According to Bulgarian law, a co-operative association is a society of natural persons built on the basis of free will, co-operative property, mutual aid and collaboration. The co-operative associations operate on the principle of self-accountability.

A member of a co-operative may be any individual over 16 years of age, or over 15 years of age if he/she is a pupil. They are liable only up to the amount of their contribution. The members of a co-operative organisation are the owners, proprietors, possessors and users of the co-operative property. The organisation itself conducts and organises economic activity, chooses the forms and methods of economic co-operation and maintains relations with the state budget, the banks and the market. It also decides upon the problems of structuring, staffing and management and makes voluntary decisions on mergers, acquisitions and membership of co-operative unions and associations.

Management and decision making in the co-operatives are effected by the following bodies:

- The general meeting is the supreme body of the co-operative, comprising all its members. Its functions include approval and amendment of the co-operative's statute, decisions concerning the distribution of incomes and revenues, and management of the real estate of the cooperative.

■ The managing board is elected by the general meeting. The liability of its members is unlimited. Its main obligations and tasks are the administration of the co-operative.

■ The chairman of the co-operative association is also the chairman of the managing board.

■ The supervisory board effects control over the entire activity of the co-operative and reports the results to the general meeting.

Co-operatives unite in regional, branch and national (central) co-operative unions. The co-operative unions co-ordinate the activities of their members, extend loans and provide funds. They can also organise co-operatives which perform economic activities.

Co-operatives have been permitted since April 1989 to enter into foreign trade in all forms permitted by the law. There are several specialised co-operative foreign trade organisations, but many co-operatives are reluctant to use intermediaries and try to maintain direct access to foreign markets.

PRIVATE COMPANIES

In the post-war years, the private company form has almost never been used, although the few exceptions included individual proprietorships and small-scale workers' co-operative enterprises conducting business in the field of crafts, servicing industries and agriculture.

The legal framework for private businesses has changed radically since the Trade Act was introduced. Its provisions guarantee equal legal status and equal rights to both the private and the public sectors in terms of establishment, registration, management, operations and liquidation procedures. There are also common rules for foreign economic activity and investment abroad.

Midway through 1992, about 190,000 private companies were registered in Bulgaria. In reality the number of private companies actually operating remains limited, generally confined to retail and distribution. More than 70 per cent of them are sole traders. Around 100,000 new private companies have been registered by unemployed individuals, while two-thirds of all private companies do not employ staff other than the proprietors.

Private businesses have contributed significantly to the restoration of market balance. They have expanded quickly in services, especially in transport and trade – service sectors that are closely linked to industry and agriculture (the goods-producing sectors) and thus heavily hit by the economic slump. Private businesses have also developed in the fields of education and health, which are adversely affected by tight government fiscal policy.

The share of private firms in industry production is still very small – less than 2 per cent, but is 42 per cent in trade (reported statistics do not often capture fully the private sector output).

Microeconomic efficiency in private companies is higher in comparison with the state sector. Less than 5 per cent of existing productive capital stock is used by private companies, while the value of their production accounts for 11.6 per cent of the net material product. The increase of wages and incomes is significant as wage control schemes are not applied. The development of the private sector has been hampered by the government's excessively restrictive microeconomic policy, the underdeveloped capital markets and the weakening of demand, both at home and abroad.

Private business entities are becoming increasingly active in foreign trade. The number of sole proprietorships, partnerships and private companies engaged in foreign trade transactions has increased dramatically from 3000–4000 to nearly 15,000 in less than a year. They already export goods which, until recently, were handled by state monopolies – for example, petrochemicals, pharmaceuticals, scrap ferrous and non-ferrous metals, meat and live animals, dairy products, citrus fruit, cigarettes and alcohol. The exact share of private companies in foreign trade is difficult to determine as they are not obliged to submit accounts. It is estimated that their share is about 25 per cent of total exports. Private companies have almost excluded their state competitors from the markets for medicinal herbs, mushrooms, citrus fruit, coffee, cigarettes and leather.

JOINT VENTURES

The loosening of the legal framework for foreign investment in Bulgaria has led to the establishment of a large number of joint ventures. In 1990, foreign investment in Bulgaria amounted to US$0.1 million, while in 1991 it increased to US$0.7–0.8 million. Still, the influx of foreign capital is limited. Compared with the other post-communist countries in Central Europe, foreign investment is about 10 times less intensive.

The state is attempting to foster the establishment of joint ventures. One of the main tasks of the present government is to select state firms eligible for foreign investment and to provide the relevant information to foreign investors. Most of the projects involve companies with obsolete productive stock which can be upgraded, principally in the sphere of food processing and production of consumer goods. Establishment of joint ventures is also encouraged in ferrous and non-ferrous metallurgy where six projects are currently under consideration.

THE COMMERCIAL OUTLOOK

For newly emerging private firms the main problems stem from the lack of experience in working in an international business environment. For state-owned companies, the old-style organisational and management structures, designed to implement plans rather than to adapt to dynamic market changes and pressures, continue to be serious obstacles.

Generally, managers of big state-owned Bulgarian enterprises are university graduates in a specific field of science and technology. Some are economists or have attended courses for post-graduate studies in economics, finance management or marketing. Technocratic approaches to problems still tend to have priority in the process of decision making.

Bulgarian companies are generally very willing to co-operate with foreign partners. In fact, many of them regard the establishment of joint ventures with Western firms as a matter of survival and, under the privatisation schemes, many companies will offer assets and packages of stocks for sale to foreign investors. These companies expect in turn to import components and spare parts for existing capital stock as well as to introduce new technologies, develop new products, obtain better access to world markets, implement Western-style management techniques and structures, and improve wage scales.

Bulgarian companies are aware that working with foreign partners requires better organisation, discipline, and higher quality standards. One of the myths accompanying the expected inflow of foreign capital is that 'financially powerful foreign investors are going to buy out the country itself'.

Bureaucracy is a major problem when doing business with Bulgaria. As stated earlier, the Council of Ministers has concentrated all its functions and competence on enterprise restructuring. All decisions concerning demonopolisation, the breaking up of enterprises, the establishment of new ones and the appointing of executive staff are extremely centralised. Bureaucracy stems from state ownership and will continue to be predominant until the restructuring process results in the creation of a viable and dominant private sector.

COMMUNICATING

European standards for business communication are generally applied in Bulgaria. Hours of work for government agencies and companies are from 8.00am till 6.00pm from Monday to Friday. Arrangements for business meetings should be made in advance and appointments should be confirmed at least 24 hours in advance.

Business contacts can be restricted by difficulties in obtaining public services, mainly telecommunication connections. Telephone and telefax lines are, however, generally available to companies active in foreign trade. The Central Post Office and a number of business centres, trade promotion organisations, agencies and consulting companies can also offer such facilities. Several international courier companies such as DHL, In-time Courier and EMES operate in Bulgaria. Numerous exhibitions, business conferences, fairs and presentations of companies' products are organised in order to encourage business contacts.

Companies might negotiate for one and the same project in parallel with several foreign partners and try to prolong the deal intentionally. A number of them have limited experience in business communications with foreign partners. They might fail to inform a foreign partner in time even when their offer is fully accepted. Generally, all forms of verbal and written communication take more time compared to Western standards.

The early stages of communicating with prospective Bulgarian business partners may be relatively simple. However, as the deal advances and becomes more detailed, they can become more cautious and hesitate for the following reasons:

- the legislation is changing very rapidly and they may need consulting assistance;

- they have limited financial power and limited access to finance;

- they lack knowledge of the foreign partner;

- they are uncertain of how to approach certain more specific parts of the deal; and

- bureaucratic delay.

English is the most commonly spoken foreign language in Bulgarian business practice, although German, French and Russian are also widespread. There are no impediments for providing a business assistant, secretary or interpreter. The more educated and younger managers have a good standard of business English. None the less some specific and new business terms should be discussed in order to avoid the possibility of any misunderstanding.

5

Market Intelligence

Touche Ross

As Bulgaria embarks on the road to a market economy there remains a lack of sufficient, reliable and timely market surveys and forecasts.

The Ministry of Foreign Economic Relations, which had much information at its disposal, was recently closed down, as were several information institutes. Those still functioning are preoccupied with financial difficulties and reorganisation plans. The passage from a planned to a free market economy has also required modifications in the methodology and techniques of data collection. However, market intelligence can be obtained through the channels outlined below.

Research capabilities, particularly in the field of agriculture, will eventually increase with the implementation of the PHARE programme in Bulgaria. It foresees a reorganisation of the National Institute of Statistics and the creation of an Export Trade Advisory Centre to monitor the service of supply and demand of basic agricultural products, and providing an agricultural market information service. The activities of the EC experts will aim at the more efficient supply and dissemination of market information and assistance in promoting Bulgarian exports.

NATIONAL INSTITUTE OF STATISTICS

The National Institute of Statistics (NIS) is to be reorganised to reflect the following:

- territorial adjustments;
- changes in production patterns resulting from the privatisation of state farming;

■ the organisation of statistical data, change of contents, models of data collection and processing and data automation systems.

The overall aim is to achieve compatibility with EC statistics. However, existing statistics can be relied upon to some extent since any discrepancies are likely to result from differences in methodology and economic categories used in the past. The NIS publishes a number of year books, guides and manuals of Bulgarian statistics.

For the last three years the NIS has been collecting annual statistical data about the role of private business in the economy, including data concerning incomes, funds, employed persons, credits, transport facilities, etc. Until now, however, only about 30 per cent of private businessmen have provided statistical information about their activities.

The available statistical publications of the NIS are numerous and cover a wide range of subjects. Some publications can be obtained in English at comparatively low prices.

MARKET SURVEYS

Conducting market surveys is complicated at present by the rapid economic and sociological changes taking place in the country. For example the wholesale distribution organisation which existed until recently has been eliminated and every producer now has direct access to the market. Thus it would presently be quite difficult to collect data or explain the functioning of the distribution network in Bulgaria.

The same applies to the collection of data concerning the production sector, now prepared for privatisation and under pressure from prohibitive interest rates (raised from 4.5 per cent to 55 per cent), devaluation of the lev, the general lack of financial means and reduction in demand. Recent consumer activity gives grounds for supposing that market research by standard methods would be possible in the medium term. For the time being, factors such as shortage of goods, imbalance between supply and demand, a fall in solvent demand, very frequent reorganisations in all fields and changes in legislation should be taken into account.

The primary sources of information for market researchers are statistics, periodicals and specialised journals. Even more important for collecting data about Bulgarian companies are direct personal contacts with specialists, working in different branches. With the frequent changes mentioned earlier taking place, the updating of information is very important.

Interviews with consumers have not so far been widely used in research, although certain institutes have specialised interviewers at their disposal. There is experience in building up computer networks of information and databases within the various ministries.

MARKET RESEARCH CAPABILITIES

Until recently, large state enterprises had departments for market research as did large state institutes, specialised by branch. However, the number of these organisations has been reduced and the remaining ones meet with difficulties typical of the transitional period – reduction in personnel, movement to a self-supporting basis, difficulties in subscribing to a sufficient number of foreign periodicals, lack of financial means and difficulty in contacting potential customers. For information services on the home market, a further problem is the lack of solvent consumers. Information services have for many years been supplied free of charge by state institutes, who are now providing them as a valuable and remunerative service.

Many of the newly founded firms in Bulgaria declare information services and market surveys to be within their sphere of activity. However, the enthusiasm of such firms appears to be much greater than their actual abilities. Most of them wish to be able to work in this field in future and, in the meantime, deal in quite different lines of business.

Other information companies and institutes have at their disposal qualified personnel, computer technology, databases and even a tradition in the field of market research. Their main problem is getting in touch with potential foreign or Bulgarian customers. Any of these institutes and organisations would be pleased and well equipped to supply all necessary information or could assist in finding the right partner.

INFORMATION SOURCES ON COMPANIES

■ The British Embassy in Sofia offers information through its Trade Department. Information in the UK is available through the Bulgarian Embassy. A new economic counsellor has been appointed to the embassy in the UK and an Anglo-Bulgarian Chamber of Commerce in London is being set up in February

1993 under the auspices of the embassy. The Bulgarian Trade Department was closed down recently as a result of the liquidation of the Ministry of Foreign Economic Relations in Bulgaria although this may be reopened in the future.

■ The Bulgarian Chamber of Commerce and Industry in Sofia and its regional branches in the larger towns (Bourgas, Varna, Veliko Turnovo, Vidin, Dobrich, Mihailovgrad, Pernik, Pleven, Plovdiv, Razgrad and Russe) is a public organisation of state, co-operative and private companies, banks and institutes.

■ The Chamber of Commerce organises Bulgaria's participation in world exhibitions and fairs as well as the annual Plovdiv trade fair. It offers legal and other consulting services to Bulgarian and foreign partners, organises seminars, conferences and presentations of foreign partners and has an official register of the private firms dealing in foreign trade. The Chamber also operates several specialised bureaux including the Bureau for Patents and Trade Marks and a Consulting Bureau. The following mixed Chambers of Commerce also exist: Arab–Bulgarian, Bulgarian–Russian, Bugarian–Yugoslav, Italo–Bulgarian, Swiss–Bulgarian, as well as the American–Bulgarian Trade Economic Council. The annual international trade fair in the city of Plovdiv was first held in 1892. The fair takes place in spring for light industry and in autumn for heavy industry. It is a member of the Association of International Fairs. Bulgaria also has several fair agencies abroad including Interfair Bulgaria Ltd in London.

■ Interpred World Trade Centre in Sofia deals in the representation of foreign companies; research, economic information and consultancy; the provision of information on leading companies; translation and Bulgarian language courses, education programmes; and office space for tenants. The Bulgarian Industrial Association assists direct contact between foreign and Bulgarian companies, including tenders for Western consultancies; advice for Western businessmen on a wide range of questions concerning the Bulgarian economy; and organises exhibitions and seminars.

■ The Scientific Institute for International Co-operation and Foreign Economic Activities deals in marketing research, foreign trade information and consultancy services, as well as the establishment of business contacts and services to foreign partners. The Institute has at its disposal qualified specialists, a library of economic literature and international statistics, databases on Bulgaria's foreign trade since 1970 and company information. The Institute publishes various bulletins in Bulgarian and English on world markets, prices and marketing. During the past two years it has sent its quarterly *Forecast of the Development of the World Economy and Markets* to the Association of the European Institutes. The customers of the Institute are mainly private companies, Bulgarian state bodies and an increasing number of foreign partners. It is included in the PHARE programme.

■   The Institute of Marketing should also be mentioned, since it has a network of 800 interviewers throughout the country. It gives information to state bodies and private firms about products and markets and organises marketing and management courses.

■   The Institute for the Development of Industry has experience in databases and market research and will soon be included in the PHARE programme for data collection.

The *National Guide* of 8000 Bulgarian companies, institutes and organisations (1991) may also be helpful, giving names, addresses and concise information. *Yellow Pages* in Bulgarian and English is also a useful guide on companies and other organisations.

Bulgarian business publications printed in English include: *Bulgarian Business News*, edited by 168 Hours Ltd; *Bank Review* – a quarterly journal edited by The National Bank of Bulgaria (first issued in 1908); *Bulgarian Economic Review* – a fortnightly publication; *Bulgarian Economic Outlook*; *Bulgarian Feature Weekly*; and *Daily News*, published by the Bulgarian Telegraph Agency (BTA). The BTA also publishes 16 editions in Bulgarian on a variety of subjects including: *Balkan Business*, containing business offers and advertisements; *Svetovni Stokovi Borsi* on the world commodity exchanges; *Svetovna Iconomica I Turgovia* on the world economy and trade; the guide *Bulgaria 1992*, with names and addresses of various organisations and institutes; and the guide *Banki I Firmi v Bulgaria* with information about banks, brokerage houses, companies, joint ventures, etc.

Economic journals and newspapers of interest in Bulgarian are: *Iconomicheski Zhivot* (Economic Life); *Pari* (Money); *Delovi Sviat*

(Business World); *Bulgarski Business* (Bulgarian Business); *Iconomicheska Misul* (Economic Thought); *Iconomichesko Regulirane* (Economic Regulation); *Mezhdunarodni Otnoshenia* (International Relations); *Infobusiness* (with offers from Bulgarian and foreign firms and foreign trade information); *168 Chasa* (168 Hours) – a widely-read weekly newspaper; *Export Business* – a monthly publication about management, forecasts, partners, markets; *Economica*; and *Borsov Biuletin* – an official publication of the Sofia commodity exchange with offers and analyses.

The *State Gazette* is also a valuable resource since it contains all the normative Acts and newly approved legislation.

DATABASES

At the Central Institute for Software Products and Systems (CISPS) an integrated automated system provides information services to companies using a wide range of package products. The Institute has, since 1983, been connected by a telecommunications network with Radio Austria, through which it enters various networks. Thanks to these databases, large information centres are used such as DIALOG, DATASTAR, QUESTEL, STN and INFOLINE.

The information technology used is increasing with the building of the national electronic network INFOTEL, and the Bulgarian Chamber of Commerce's automated INFOBUSINESS system which provides exchange of trade offers for sales, joint ventures and co-operation.

6

Trading Partners
Sinclair Roche & Temperley

This chapter outlines the development of Bulgarian foreign trade in recent years. The main hallmarks of Bulgaria's development are the relative decline of agriculture and the growth of industry during the period of communist rule. Within Comecon, Bulgaria had the highest dependence on the Soviet Union as an export market and in planning its industrial structure was highly integrated into the Comecon trading system. The country now faces a major challenge in finding new export markets and upgrading or replacing outdated industrial plant.

THE EARLY DEVELOPMENT OF INDUSTRY AND TRADE

Until after World War II, Bulgaria was a predominantly agricultural country, and its industry (initially mainly food processing) was slow to develop. Before World War I, almost 80 per cent of trade was in food and drink. The leading export markets were the Ottoman Empire and France; wheat was the main export to Western Europe. Leading importers were Austria-Hungary, Britain and, increasingly, Germany.

Tobacco, which was given a kick-start in World War I, remained a leading export earner in the inter-war period, while wheat exports declined. A rapid growth in internal textile production, in part forced by the Depression, led to its replacing food processing as the biggest industry, comprising 65 per cent of total industrial production by 1931. During this period, 15 per cent of industry and banking capital was in foreign hands, though this figure declined in the 1930s.

The inter-war period was also characterised by an increasing dependence on Germany. By 1939, Germany was taking 67.8 per cent of Bulgaria's total exports, and also providing 65.6 per cent of total imports. Five years later the figures were 87.7 per cent and 72.2 per cent respectively.

BULGARIA'S ECONOMIC DEVELOPMENT WITHIN COMECON

The period after World War II saw radical changes in the Bulgarian economy. Not only did industrial production rapidly increase (as late as 1938 it had only comprised 5.6 per cent of GNP), but trade allegiances were switched almost overnight as the communists staged a coup in 1944. Although the communists did not consolidate their power for another three years, trade with the Soviet Union was intensive from the start, dictated by an arrangement by which the USSR bought Bulgarian goods at 1933 prices. Under a 1947 agreement, Soviet cotton, rubber, motor vehicles and machinery were traded for Bulgarian tobacco. Not surprisingly, trade relations in the immediate post-war years were dominated by the Soviet bloc, which in 1951 absorbed 93 per cent of exports and supplied 93 per cent of imports.

However, later years were to see a modest revival of trade with West Germany, which provided 8.2 per cent of total imports in 1959, and in 1975 the two countries concluded a 10-year economic co-operation agreement.

Meanwhile, a series of five-year plans from 1949 onwards were rapidly, if painfully, transforming the economy. The creation of collective farms was probably the least successful aspect of this process, causing widespread dissent and disrupting the social fabric. In 1958, by which time collectivisation had been completed and the economy was relatively speaking prospering, a new plan to create even larger units – agro-industrial complexes – once more disrupted the countryside. However, small-holdings continued to survive, albeit on a small scale and in a different guise: families were allowed control over the produce from individual parcels of land though not owner-ship of the land itself. It was recently estimated that these small-holdings accounted for 40 per cent of total agricultural produce.

In contrast to the overall decline of agriculture, industrial production developed rapidly, so that by 1969 it engaged 82 per cent of the labour-force. Initially the emphasis was on heavy industry. The Soviet Union took over a number of pre-war German and Italian ventures and, in addition, a number of Soviet–Bulgarian joint companies were created in, for example, lead and zinc processing and the extraction of uranium. The late-1950s saw the birth of the petrochemical industry, based almost exclusively at Bourgas on the Black Sea coast, where crude oil was imported (mainly from the USSR) and processed in a number of ways.

As the command economy developed and integration and rationalisation of economic production within Comecon increased, Bulgaria began to specialise in various areas. In particular there was an emphasis on the production of transport goods in the years 1965–75 and, increasingly from the 1970s onwards, Bulgaria established a reputation in the computer industry. At the same time, the Black Sea coast was being rapidly developed as a centre for mass tourism. In the late 1970s and 1980s, along with tourism, wine and computers, there was heavy investment in the machine-tool industry.

Along with many other Comecon countries, Bulgaria had considerable problems in the 1970s in financing its debts to the West which rose to US$11 billion by 1991. At the same time, Bulgaria had over the years expanded its contacts within Comecon, not just relying on Soviet trade. In time of labour surplus it had been heavily involved in third world training programmes in Comecon countries, and had also increased its trade links with North Africa and the Middle East to the extent that, in 1981, Libya became its third largest trading partner (after the USSR and the GDR).

TRADE IN THE 1990s

The collapse of Comecon affected Bulgaria more than any other Eastern European country, given its particular dependence on Soviet trade. Previous agreements have had to be renegotiated, with an emphasis on barter due to the need to conserve hard currency reserves. In February 1992, an agreement was signed with Russia providing for a clearing system for trade in particular commodities. Imports from Russia include crude oil and natural gas; exports to Russia consist of cigarettes, medicines, food, meat and soda ash. Payments are made into authorised accounts in dollars at agreed exchange rates. The credit limit has been set at US$100 million.

While it is estimated that trade with former Comecon countries declined by as much as 70 per cent during 1991, Bulgarian tobacco exports have at least remained largely unaffected, and the general trade situation is now likely to stabilise. It is still important for

Bulgaria to maintain close trading contacts with Russia and the Ukraine. A new 10-year friendship treaty was signed between Russia and Bulgaria in August 1992 on which occasion the Russian President appeared to rate Bulgaria behind only the USA and Japan as a future trading partner.

Negotiations for associate membership of the EC began in May 1992 and were expected to be completed within the year. In 1990, EC countries imported US$760 million worth of goods from Bulgaria, and exports amounted to US$1.15 billion. The EC has recently agreed to fund an ECU11.5 million project to improve safety at the Kozlodui nuclear power station.

The World Bank is considering a US$75 million loan to support a project aimed at improving electricity distribution in Bulgaria and other power generation projects are being developed by Bechtel Power Corporation, backed by the US Trade and Development Programme, with possible funding from the World Bank and EBRD. Negotiations for membership of GATT have also begun (Bulgaria currently has observer status). The outcome will largely depend on how quickly the country can comply with GATT regulations concerning competition, tariffs, dumping, etc.

Bulgaria's growing trade with Libya has been hard hit by Bulgaria joining in international sanctions against Libya. Serious losses have also been caused by sanctions against Iraq in the recent Gulf War. Losses, directly or indirectly, from sanctions against Serbia are estimated at US$60 million per month. The embargo on Serbia has led both Bulgaria and Romania, among the countries most affected, to seek closer ties.

The IMF appeared recently to be close to agreeing a US$660 million support programme for Bulgaria, but the failure to reach agreement on a rescheduling of the country's commercial debt has seriously impeded trade. Virtually no Western banks are prepared to back credits for the supply of goods to Bulgaria, and export credit insurers are similarly reluctant to extend cover for exports on deferred payment terms. There is at the same time some hope that CoCom restrictions on the export of optic and polymer fibre telecommunications systems to Bulgaria may shortly be removed to enable the country's outdated telecommunications systems to be modernised. Bulgaria has received commitments of US$150 million from lending institutions to support this US$230 million project.

Recent trade statistics (see Table 6.1) have shown a significant increase in trade with Turkey, which is expected by many observers to be destined to play an increasingly important role in the area.

Table 6.1 *Exports to and imports from Western countries, 1990–91 (US$m: annual totals)*

	Exports		Imports	
	1990	1991	1990	1991
Germany	247	322	485	482
Yugoslavia	158	239*	102	234*
Italy	156	175	268	248
Greece	114	156	53	88
France	84	100	116	191
USA	67	56	84	142
UK	59	65	80	62
Netherlands	32	40*	61	48*
Turkey	32	128*	11	64*
Austria	49	52	122	119

* Estimates

Between 1990 and 1991, exports to Turkey increased from US$32 million to US$128 million, while imports increased from US$11 million to US$64 million. Poverty and unemployment in regions populated by ethnic Turks have resulted in an exodus of an estimated 80,000 Turkish Bulgarians, and the condition of the ethnic Turkish population is now causing political tension having regard to the ability of the party representing the Turkish population to decide the delicate balance between the main political parties; the situation may affect the attitude of the Turkish government toward trade relations with Bulgaria.

7

Foreign Investment

Sinclair Roche & Temperley

Even though there now appears to be no turning back from the reform process after the October 1991 elections, the transformation of Bulgaria's former command economy will be a drawn-out process. Everyday life, customary practices and deeply rooted ideas associated with the old regime must change. This process will be a bigger and more time consuming task than legislative and administrative reform. It is to be hoped that foreign investment will act as a catalyst, speeding up the reform process by bringing with it, as well as much needed funds, exposure to new technological and financial skills, Western style management and training and, above all, interaction with foreign businessmen.

Foreign investment in Bulgaria was initially made possible by Decree 56 on Economic Activity of January 1989. This Decree reformed investment regulation and afforded substantial new rights in Bulgaria to foreign individuals and companies. Decree 56 was substantially superseded by the Foreign Investment Act of May 1991.

The most significant step in introducing new free market oriented foreign investment legislation came after the October 1991 elections with the repeal of the May 1991 Act and the enactment of the Law on the Economic Activity of Foreign Persons and on the Protection of Foreign Investments (the 'FIL'). This became effective as of 1 February 1992.

WHAT IS A FOREIGN INVESTMENT?

For the purpose of the FIL, any investment which is made by a foreign person or by a company in which the level of foreign participation exceeds 50 per cent is considered a foreign investment.

Thus, a Bulgarian registered company in which the majority of shares is owned by a foreign person qualifies as a foreign investor. Similarly, ownership of real estate in Bulgaria by a company with more than 50 per cent foreign participation is considered as foreign investment and is governed by the FIL.

Under the FIL, a foreign person is an entity or a company or a natural person resident or registered abroad. Bulgarian citizens who have another citizenship must choose which status they wish to use in their business activities. Once chosen, the status cannot be changed.

RESTRICTIONS ON INVESTMENT

The list of foreign investments requiring approval contained in the former Foreign Investment Act of 1991 has been considerably shortened by the FIL. Permission for foreign investments is needed in the following fields:

1. manufacture of and trade in arms, ammunition and military equipment;

2. carrying on of banking and insurance and acquisition of interests in banks and insurance companies;

3. acquisition of immovable property in geographical areas designated by the Council of Ministers;

4. exploration, exploitation and extraction of natural resources from the territorial sea, the continental shelf or the exclusive economic zone; and

5. acquisition of an interest which will secure a majority in decision making or block decision making in an enterprise carrying on a business or owning property for which permission under the law is required.

Transactions conducted in contravention of the FIL through an intermediary may be invalidated by a court ruling on a submission by a public prosecutor or the interested parties. Should this be the case, the state has the right to seize the property contributed by the parties.

Where required, permits are issued by the Council of Ministers or a body authorised by it (apart from permits for investment related to banking and insurance which are to be issued by the Governing

Board of the National Bank of Bulgaria). The Council of Ministers advertises in the *Official Gazette* the conditions to be met for the issue of a permit. The application must be approved or rejected within 45 days of its submission (except for banking and insurance, where the National Bank must act within 6 months in response to an application to carry on such business or 3 months where an acquisition of an interest in such business is concerned). Reasons must be given for the rejection of an application.

Even though the activity in which the foreign investor wishes to engage is permitted by the FIL, for certain business activities (including registration as a sole trader, acquisition of an interest in a co-operative and acquisition of an interest in a general partnership) a foreign person must obtain a Bulgarian residence permit.

INVESTMENTS IN REAL ESTATE

Bulgarian law distinguishes between title to and rights to use land on the one hand, and buildings erected on the land on the other. Foreign persons, as defined by the FIL, may acquire rights of ownership in buildings and limited real rights in immovable property. However, a foreign person may acquire houses or apartments only if the building in which the dwelling is situated is built by him or the acquisition is carried out according to special statutory procedures. According to Article 5(i) of the FIL, a foreign person may not acquire a right of ownership in land as such through a branch or as a sole trader. Should the holding of non-agricultural land be a paramount objective of a foreign investor, the safest course is to incorporate a Bulgarian private company as the vehicle for the purchase of the land. It is possible for a Bulgarian company with majority foreign participation to acquire Bulgarian non-agricultural land.

TYPES OF INVESTMENT VEHICLE

There are four types of vehicle available to foreign investors:

1. a branch or representative office;

2. an enterprise formed under the Bulgarian Commercial Law;

3. a joint venture; and

4. an agency or distributorship.

The minimum investment of US$50,000 required under the Foreign Investment Act of May 1991 has now been abolished by the FIL. A minimum capital of Lev50,000 (approximately US$2500) is required to be deposited with a Bulgarian bank before a Bulgarian private limited company can be registered.

Any foreign person has the right to open a commercial agency in Bulgaria by registration at the Bulgarian Chamber of Commerce and Industry. Such agencies have no separate legal personality and may not carry on business other than the representation of the foreign principal.

SECURITY, REPATRIATION AND INVESTMENT PROTECTION

Although it has always been possible to mortgage land under Bulgarian law, a mortgage could not hitherto be granted to a foreigner. Under Article 12 of the FIL, however, both pledge and mortgage have been introduced as forms of security available to foreign investors. In such cases, contrary to the Law of Obligations and Contracts, a pledge will be valid even if the object remains in the physical possession of the debtor. The security must be in the form of notarial deed. It must, however, be noted that the enforcement of a mortgage cannot result in the acquisition by a foreign person of land which cannot itself be owned by him.

Rules relating to repatriation of revenue and foreign exchange are quite liberal. Practically no restrictions are now imposed. The lev is now internally convertible and foreigners are entitled to exchange lev income into hard currency and transfer the proceeds abroad. As a matter of practice, however, the conversion of leva into foreign currency through an authorised Bulgarian bank can be subject to substantial delay.

According to the FIL, property in Bulgaria owned by a foreigner may not be expropriated by the state except for exceptionally important state needs that cannot be satisfied in any other way. Compensation, either in cash or in kind, equal to the full market value must be made. Expropriation can be effected only on the grounds of parliamentary laws and must be specifically approved by an order of the Minister of Finance. Both expropriation and compensation are subject to appeal before the Supreme Court. Bulgaria has entered into a number of investment protection treaties with major Western trading nations.

CONCLUSION

Overall, foreign investment legislation in Bulgaria is now quite liberal and the law contains similar protections and incentives to those of the other former Comecon (CMEA) countries which have set out to encourage foreign investment. The initially very cautious provisions of Decree 56 of 1989, which tried to fit foreign investment into an essentially communist economic framework and the less socialist but nevertheless flawed provisions of the May 1991 Foreign Investment Act, have now been almost totally swept away by the FIL, which represents a strong political statement in favour of foreign investment as a means of revitalising Bulgaria's economy.

Part II

The Business Infrastructure

8

Commercial Law

Sinclair Roche & Temperley

Bulgarian commercial law is contained principally in the Law on Obligations and Contracts of 5 December 1950, as amended (the 'LOC'), which was based upon and updated from the Bulgarian Civil Code of 1892. The LOC was the product of a communist government and still contains references to state enterprises and social planning. These references have now been deleted. The LOC has more recently been supplemented by the Commercial Law of 16 May 1991 (the 'Commercial Law'), the Law on the Economic Activity of Foreign Persons and on the Protection of Foreign Investments of 16 January 1992 (the 'FIL') and the Fair Competition Law of 17 May 1991 (the 'FCL').

The Commercial Law enacts provisions relating to the conduct of trade, companies, other legal persons and agency, and is more particularly summarised in Chapters 21 and 25. The FIL has already been dealt with extensively in Chapter 7. This chapter will concentrate on the LOC and the FCL.

THE LAW OF CONTRACT

The LOC lays down the general principle of freedom of contract provided there is no breach of the law and public policy is not offended.

Formation of the contract

In pre-contractual negotiations the parties must act in good faith and failure to do so can result in damages being awarded to the innocent party. A contract is formed by offer and acceptance but consideration is not an important element in a valid contract. There is no specific form for a contract under Bulgarian law, except for one in respect of immovable property which must be by notarial deed.

The terms and conditions

The parties are free to set the terms and conditions of their contract except that terms limiting liability for gross negligence are invalid. In interpreting a contract the law looks to the common intention of the parties to determine the applicable terms. Even express terms will be interpreted by reference to the whole transaction, its object, custom and practice and the overriding principle of good faith.

The LOC treats as void contracts in breach of the law or offensive to public policy, those the object of which is impossible and those not in a form required by law (eg a contract for the sale of land which is not by notarial deed). Certain types of contracts are voidable at the instance of the innocent party, eg those concluded by a person lacking legal capacity, those concluded by a representative acting outside his authority and those where there is an element of mistake, fraud or undue influence. On this basis, a party encouraged to enter into a contract by a serious misrepresentation may be entitled to avoid the contract.

Remedies for breach of contract

The principal remedies for breach of contract under the LOC are specific performance (eg payment of the price or delivery of the goods purchased) and/or damages for non-performance.

Damages compensate the actual loss sustained and the loss of bargain to the extent that these are the direct and foreseeable consequences of the breach. The exception is where there is bad faith on the part of the party in breach, in which case he is responsible to compensate all immediate and direct losses. Where the breach is due to circumstances outside a party's control, the court may reduce the damages or exempt the party from paying damages altogether. Furthermore the innocent party must take steps to mitigate his loss in good faith. Where there has been a breach of a payment obligation, the guilty party is also responsible for statutory interest on the outstanding amount until it is paid in full. Other remedies provided by the LOC include rescission, an unpaid seller's lien over goods and a right of set-off.

Contracts for the sale of goods

The LOC provides that a seller of goods must deliver them to the buyer in the same condition as they were at the time of sale, together with all benefits accruing thereto, and give good title in the goods to the buyer.

The seller will be liable for defects which substantially reduce the value of the goods or their fitness for normal use. However, the seller is not liable for latent defects or defects of which the buyer was aware. Where the seller is liable, the buyer may either return the goods and claim repayment of the price and damages or keep the goods and claim a reduction in the price and/or demand that the seller rectifies the defect. The buyer's rights may be limited if he did not inspect the goods carefully or if the defect was caused by him.

If the seller does not give good title, the buyer may rescind the contract and claim repayment of the price and damages, unless he was aware of the defective title. A buyer's rights on a breach of contract for the sale of goods lapse after one year, or six months from delivery in the case of immovable and movable goods, respectively.

Under the LOC, the buyer must pay the price for the goods on delivery. The seller may rescind the contract if the price is not paid as and when agreed.

It is worth noting that Bulgarian law does not recognise a retention of title clause for the protection of the seller, except in the case of a contract for the hire purchase of movable goods, where the seller may retain title to the goods until the final instalment is paid.

SECURITY

The LOC recognises the concepts of suretyship, pledge and mortgage as means of securing the performance of a debtor's obligations. This may be of particular importance to a foreign investor who is financing activities in Bulgaria and who wishes to take security from his Bulgarian borrower or joint venture party.

The rights of foreign investors have been substantially improved by Article 12 of the FIL which now provides that:

1. a foreign investor's claim either in leva or in a foreign currency may be secured by a pledge or mortgage;

2. provided that there is a written contract with an authentic date, such a pledge is valid even where the pledged asset remains in the possession and control of the debtor; and

3. no state permission is required for the conclusion of such a mortgage.

Contracts of suretyship

These must be in writing and the LOC provides that the guarantor is jointly liable with the debtor for the performance of the secured obligation. The debtor is obliged to notify the guarantor promptly upon satisfaction of the debt. If the guarantor satisfies the debt he becomes subrogated to the rights of the creditor against the debtor.

Pledge

A pledge is a method whereby security is taken over movable assets and monetary claims. The LOC provides that a pledge is only valid if the pledged asset is transferred to the creditor or a nominee on his behalf. Article 12 of the FIL varies this provision, at least in so far as a pledge in favour of a foreign investor is concerned. The creditor must not use the pledged asset and must keep it safely and in good condition. Upon enforcement, the creditor may not sell the pledged asset without a court order, unless it is a bank.

Mortgage

The LOC provides that a mortgage is the means of taking security over immovable property. It must be created by a notarial deed and must be registered at the local Notarial Office. A mortgage must be over a specific property and to secure a specific sum and accordingly the deed of mortgage must specify the owner of the property, the debtor (if other than the owner), the creditor, the sum secured, an accurate description of the property and details of the claim, including the maturity date and the rate of interest. Failure to specify these matters may result in the nullity of the mortgage on grounds of uncertainty.

Registration protects a mortgage for 10 years unless the registration is renewed prior to expiry of that period. A mortgagee is a preferred creditor in respect of the mortgaged property, but he may only realise his security by sale at a public auction.

OTHER PROVISIONS IN THE LOC

The LOC comprises 436 articles and it is impossible to summarise it in detail here. In addition to dealing with contractual obligations, the sale of goods and security, the LOC also makes specific provision for loans, deposits, production contracts, assignments, commission and forwarding contracts, contracts of carriage and insurance and negotiable instruments.

COMPETITION LAW

As in the case of other former communist states, Bulgaria was quick to enact the FCL as a reaction against the monopolistic tendencies of a controlled economy and as a first step towards the establishment of a market economy. The objects of the law are to provide conditions for free enterprise, free market prices and consumer protection, together with remedies against monopoly abuse and unfair competition. It will be interesting to see how the law is implemented in practice, especially in view of both the desperate need to encourage foreign investment in Bulgaria and the stated policy of privatisation of state industries.

The FCL is administered by the Commission for the Protection of Competition (the 'CPC'), an independent body created by the law and funded by the government's annual budget.

Monopolies

The FCL prohibits monopolies whether they are established by the state or municipal authorities, or whether they are abused by other parties carrying out activities which restrict competition or harm the interests of consumers. A monopoly exists where a person:

1. has a legal right exclusively to conduct a particular economic activity (such as production, service, trade, agency, credit, insurance, etc); or

2. independently or jointly with others has a market share of more than 35 per cent in a particular economic activity.

State authorities are specifically prohibited from creating monopolies by amalgamating or incorporating enterprises. Other examples of monopolies prohibited by the law include:

■ activities restricting others from developing the market or access thereto;

■ the application of unequal contractual terms, including unnecessary restrictions or increased liabilities;

■ the creation of artificial limitations on the supply of goods;

- the imposition of irrelevant contractual conditions; and
- the fixing of unrealistic prices for long periods.

Restrictive agreements

The FCL prohibits:

1. agreements and decisions which either expressly or tacitly provide for or result in the creation of a monopoly in Bulgaria;

2. contractual terms restricting the choice of market or the source or target of supply, unless they are the natural consequence of the type of contract and do not harm the interests of consumers; and

3. exclusivity agreements which either lead to a restriction of competition in Bulgaria or to the establishment of a monopoly.

The CPC may authorise restrictive agreements if they do not affect the unregulated determination of prices, restrict competition or harm the interest of consumers.

Unfair competition

The FCL prohibits unfair competition as any economic action or practice which offends good faith and normal commercial practice and damages or may damage the interests of competitors in their relations either with the person carrying on the activity or with consumers. The law gives some examples, including:

- damaging the reputation of a competitor by misrepresentation;
- misdescription of a competitor's goods or services;
- misleading advertising;
- passing off; and
- giving misleading information about prices or other terms and conditions of sale.

There is a strict prohibition on breaches of business confidence and against the disclosure of commercial secrets. Employees' duties of confidence both during and after their employment are particularly strict (see Chapter 18).

Remedies

The CPC may, where there is an abuse of a monopoly, either impose fixed prices or set import and export quotas on the offending party. In addition, an aggrieved party or the CPC may apply to the court for an order:

- establishing the abuse and non-compliance with the FCL;

- terminating the business;

- declaring the offensive agreement null and void;

- confiscating any resulting profits; and

- imposing fines of between Lev5000 (US$250) and Lev1,000,000 (US$45,000).

9

Currency Convertibility

SG Warburg

Until 1989, the foreign exchange market consisted of an official market in which the Lev/US dollar rate was set at an artificially high level of 0.84; and a black market in which the rate was 8–10 higher. In 1989 an auction system was established whereby foreign exchange earnings could be sold directly between Bulgarian enterprises. The condition for applying for foreign exchange was that the firm produce goods for 'people's needs'. In August 1989, the lowest rate which an enterprise was prepared to sell was Lev8.25 to the US dollar and the highest rate which a firm was prepared to pay was Lev16 to the US dollar.

THE 1990 PARTIAL LIBERALISATION

In April 1990 in response to Bulgaria's increasing balance of payments deficit, the Lukanov administration took a number of measures aimed at partial liberalisation of the foreign exchange regime. A system of three exchange rates was established consisting of:

1. a basic rate set at Lev3 to the US dollar, applying to foreign debt repayment and to a small number of basic goods and invisibles;

2. a cash rate of Lev7.2 to the US dollar applying to purchases of bank notes and travellers cheques; and

3. a market rate set by monthly auctions and applying to all remaining transactions. This rate was set at Lev7.06 to the US dollar in the June 1990 auction.

In addition, firms were allowed to retain 50 per cent of net foreign exchange earnings, provided they surrendered the remainder to the

Bulgarian Foreign Trade Bank ('BFTB'). They were also permitted to obtain foreign exchange from other firms at a company auction.

The resulting devaluation of the Lev was designed to give firms an incentive to export. However, the reform proved insufficient to generate significant shifts in production. Moreover, the system quickly faced supply constraints, as very few firms made their foreign exchange earnings available during the auctions. As a result, only US$30 million were offered at the May and June auction, and only US$1.5 million at the May company auction. Due to the scarcity of foreign currency, no further auctions took place from June 1990 and firms found themselves restricted from importing as much as they required. In addition, foreign exchange rates did not reflect supply and demand factors since the authorities could manipulate the market substantially by releasing only small amounts of foreign exchange. There was a gradual dollarisation of the economy with parallel market transactions taking place at rates exceeding the official rate.

THE 1991 REFORM

Following the failure of the 1990 liberalisation it was acknowledged that in order to eliminate price distortions and inefficiencies, a

tpdel Table 9.1 *Foreign exchange reserves with the BNB (in millions), Aug 1991–Mar 1992*

	Currency	31 Aug 1991	30 Sept 1991	31 Oct 1991	30 Nov 1991	31 Dec 1991	31 Jan 1992	29 Feb 1992	31 Mar 1992
On current	USD	61.9	121.6	37.2	27.0	79.0	62.1	47.910	50.717
accounts	DEM	3.3	4.7	5.9	4.7	6.3	5.6	5.020	48.791
	GBP	0.1	0.2	0.3	8.0	0.6	0.9	1.000	1.084
	ECU	98.8	86.7	72.8	48.3	54.5	68.7	63.761	208.762
	ATS							0.200	0.123
	JPY								1007.399
	CHF								0.129
Deposits	USD	65.0	59.5	70.5	47.5	60.5	65.0	66.000	49.500
	DEM	19.0	9.0				3.0	3.025	44.025
	GBP	7.7	12.7	12.7	5.0	12.7	12.7	12.700	12.700
	ECU	50.0	50.0	50.0	50.0	50.0	50.0	50.500	50.500
	JPY							644.187	
Securities	ECU		5.0	20.0	25.0	20.0	7.0	13.000	13.000
bought	USD			49.0	5.0				68.000
(nominal value)	DEM								5.000

Source: Bulgarian National Bank.

unified exchange rate system was needed, while a floating rate policy was recognised as essential for the purpose of maintaining the competitiveness of Bulgarian exports.

Effective from 1 February 1991, the Council of Ministers adopted a decree unifying multiple exchange rates and introducing a decentralised framework of foreign exchange allocation based on an inter-bank market. Commercial banks were permitted to buy and sell foreign currencies against leva at freely negotiated rates to satisfy the request of their customers. The existing informal exchange market was allowed to function transparently and with minimal restrictions, provided that all transactions were channelled through the banking system. The National Bank was put in charge of supervising the market. Firms were authorised to purchase foreign exchange freely from commercial banks for settling their imports of goods and services and surrender requirements were abolished. At the same time, restrictions on allocation of foreign exchange for Bulgarian tourists travelling abroad were eased. Access to foreign exchange for profit repatriation was authorised in a liberal manner in the Foreign Investment Law of May 1991 and the remaining controls were removed in February 1992.

CURRENCY DEVELOPMENTS

The immediate impact of the foreign exchange reforms was a steep devaluation of the currency from Lev2.8 to Lev31 to the US dollar in

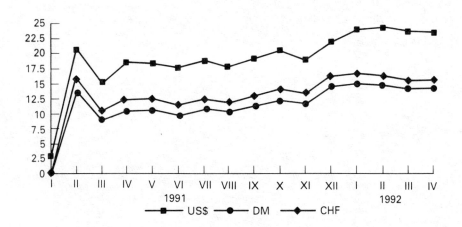

Figure 9.1   *End-month Lev exchange rates against major currencies, 1991–92*

February. Thereafter, the foreign exchange rate gradually recovered to Lev14 during the middle of March. From the end of March to the end of September the currency went from a rate of Lev15.50 to Lev18.50 to the US dollar. Short-term speculation ahead of the general and local elections in October 1991 and of the presidential elections in January 1992, as well as concerns about the amount of external financing which Bulgaria expected to receive, led to a further devaluation of the currency to approximately Lev25 to the US dollar by the year-end, having reached a record level of Lev24 in November. During 1991, interest rates and credit ceilings were used as the main policy instrument for defending the currency.

Since the start of 1992, the currency has remained almost stable with a gradual depreciation to Lev24 to the US dollar, consistent with the general appreciation of the dollar on the international markets. The depreciation of the Lev against West European currencies was less pronounced. The Bulgarian currency recovered to Lev23 to the US dollar in March and April 1992. As foreign exchange reserves built up and inflationary fears subsided, the Bulgarian currency stabilised further over the second half of 1992.

10

Prices

SG Warburg

Until 1990 Bulgaria was virtually insulated from international price developments. During the 1980s, wholesale price inflation was, on average, less than 1 per cent and retail prices were often set below wholesale prices (see Figure 10.1 showing price averages based on a basket of 168 consumer goods). Although a complex system of price controls and subsidies was effective at guaranteeing minimum living standards, it also led to major distortions in resource allocation and provided little incentive to producers to improve competitiveness.

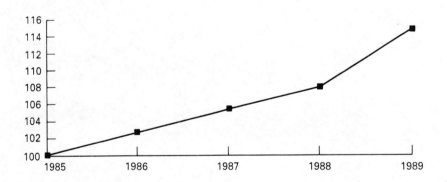

Figure 10.1 *Average retail prices in Bulgaria, 1985–89*
Source: Central Statistical Office.

THE 1990 PHASED APPROACH

In 1990 the Lukanov government acknowledged that reform was required to remedy the severe inefficiencies caused by the pricing system. The government opted for a gradual approach towards price liberalisation. In the first half of 1990, approximately 20 per cent of wholesale prices and 10 per cent of retail prices were freed, mostly in the agricultural sector. As a result, prices during the first quarter of 1990 increased by a record 9.4 per cent over the same period in 1989. Implementation of further measures was substantially delayed due to political developments. Inflation was, on average, 7 per cent per month from May to October 1990, partly due to an increase in gasoline prices of 100 per cent in July 1990, and partly due to the steep wage increases that were granted in the first quarter of 1990. For the year as a whole, retail prices increased by 70 per cent.

THE 1991 REFORM

The government's gradual approach towards price liberalisation came under review after Bulgaria joined the IMF in September 1990. It was decided that in order for distortions to be eliminated, a wide range of reforms was necessary, with prices in all sectors to be freed at the same time.

As part of Bulgaria's economic reform programme, a radical liberalisation programme was implemented on 1 February 1991 for both producer and consumer prices. Restrictions on setting most prices were removed and it was agreed that intervention in essential areas was to take place only if price increases exceeded the projected average level of 500 per cent.

The reform included increases in prices of electricity (+420 per cent for industry and +339 per cent for consumers), heating (+817 per cent and +400 per cent), petroleum products (+270 per cent and +108 per cent), butane propane gas (+308 per cent) and coal (+1325 per cent and 650 per cent) which were designed to bring Bulgaria's energy prices into line with international levels, and to promote a more efficient use of resources. Some subsidies remained for household electricity, heating and coal, and further price increases were planned for the autumn. However, due to the sharp deterioration of the exchange rate, energy price increases ranging from 70 to 100 per cent were implemented in June, thereby eliminating virtually all subsidies.

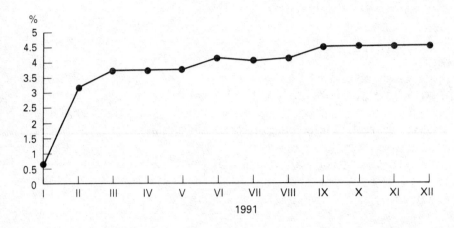

Figure 10.2   *Average monthly basic interest rates, 1991*

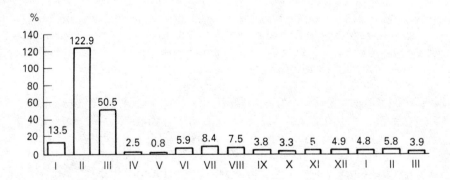

Figure 10.3   *Monthly growth of consumer prices before and after the 1991 price jump*

Source: Bulgarian National Bank.

During 1991, interest rates were the main policy instrument used by the monetary authorities to thwart hyperinflation. After their initial steep rise, interest rates were kept high throughout the year in order to ensure a positive real level for investors.

PRICE DEVELOPMENTS AND OUTLOOK

The price reform, coupled with a substantial devaluation of the Lev, had an immediate but one-off inflationary effect. Consumer price inflation was 122.9 per cent in February and 50.5 per cent in March 1991, substantially above projected levels. Although the authorities did not intervene, inflation declined to 13 per cent in March 1991 and April inflation was 3.5 per cent, with the food component declining to around 4 per cent. Reflecting, in part, energy price increases, inflation over the summer of 1991 rose from 5.9 per cent in June to 7.5 per cent in August. This rate was steadily reduced to under 4 per cent in October. Inflation for 1991 as a whole was 500 per cent. Food prices were estimated to have increased by seven to ten times since the start of the reform process.

At the end of January 1992, a temporary price freeze was announced on 14 basic commodities, including wheat, meat, dairy

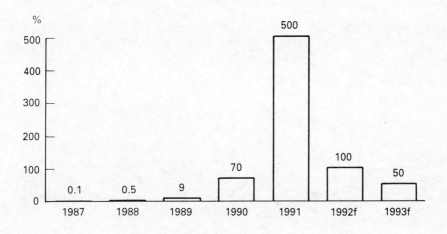

Figure 10.4 *End-year consumer prices, 1987–93*
Source: Official statistics.

products, electricity, fuel and other essentials. This measure helped contain inflation to a monthly average of 5 per cent over the first quarter of 1992, confirming the tendency observed during the last quarter of 1991. This slow but persisting level of 5 per cent is slightly higher than the 3.5 per cent target due to the depressed state of production, increases in real incomes, and the gradual depreciation of the currency.

It is generally believed that deeper structural reforms are needed to reduce inflation to target levels. These reforms include the modernisation of the banking system to stimulate non-cash payments, together with demonopolisation. The increase in competition which would result from the dismantling of large state-owned monopolies is, according to some economists, the only measure capable of bringing sustainable low inflation. New regulations passed in April 1992 on banking reform and on privatisations therefore constitute steps in the right direction.

11

The Banking System

SG Warburg

Until the late-1980s, the Bulgarian banking system's objective was to finance the needs of enterprises as per the national plan. The system was highly specialised and each participant's role was clearly defined:

1. The Bulgarian National Bank, being the central bank, received deposits from enterprises and granted credits in Lev.

2. The Bulgarian Foreign Trade Bank had a monopoly over foreign exchange operations.

3. The State Savings Bank mobilised deposits and loans to households.

Specialised banks were set up in 1987 as joint stock companies in a number of sectors including agriculture (the Agro-Cooperative Bank), transport (the Transport Bank), construction (the Stroy Bank) and electronics (the Electronics Bank), to finance investment requirements in both domestic and foreign currencies.

FIRST REFORMS

In 1981 a new bank, the Bank for Business Investments ('Mineral Bank'), was organised as a joint stock company. Its main objective was to provide financing for activities not covered by the national plan, principally in the light industries sector.

The first significant change to the banking system was introduced at the end of 1989. Former branches of the Bulgarian National Bank were transformed into commercial banks, and specialisation by product or industry was officially eliminated. All banks were allowed to receive deposits and provide credit to any economic sector, and to households. However, only the Foreign Trade Bank and the specialised banks were licensed to carry out foreign exchange operations.

While the creation of universal banks was expected to introduce a degree of competition into the banking industry, the changes were slowed down by a number of structural problems. Most of the newly created banks were very small, and the limited size of their assets was proving a major obstacle to credit activity. Commercial banks were still dependent on the Bulgarian National Bank for capital and credit decisions. Concentration on sectors and specialisation in banking products was still the rule and diversification was sometimes achieved at the expense of efficiency. Some regulatory constraints on banks' exposure were strongly needed – for instance to prevent credit to a single client from representing several times the amount of capital held by a bank.

Soon after the first reforms it was acknowledged that the modernisation of the banking sector would not be successful without substantial infusions of know-how. During 1990, the Lukanov government drafted a number of laws to liberalise the banking system further. The programme included measures to facilitate the opening of foreign banks' affiliates in Bulgaria and to remove limitations on the share of foreign participation in commercial banks. The draft law also considered that banks should set their own credit limits. Progress in the adoption of the legislation was delayed by the fall of the government in November 1990 and the structural issues were addressed again in the context of Bulgaria's economic reform programme, in February 1991.

THE RESTRUCTURING PACKAGE

In its letter of intent to the IMF of February 1991, a wide-ranging set of measures to reform the banking sector was announced, comprising the establishment of an inter-bank market for foreign exchange, and draft laws to increase the independence of the Bulgarian National Bank and to strengthen its operations.

Legislation on banking supervision, regulations on provisions and capital adequacy ratios were also submitted to Parliament. In June 1991 the Central Bank Act was adopted, establishing the independence of the Bulgarian National Bank *vis-à-vis* the government and making it accountable to Parliament only. The Bulgarian National Bank assumed full responsibility for credit, interest rate and exchange rate policies as well as supervisory functions over the banking system. During 1991, considerable efforts were made to modernise banking operations, with the technical assistance of the IMF.

In April 1992, a comprehensive package of reforms was enacted, with the following objectives:

1. the creation of a modern central banking and regulatory framework;

2. financial and institutional restructuring of the banks and the banking system; and

3. privatisation of banks.

The new Act gives the central bank extensive powers to supervise and take remedial action, including penalties against any violation. The Bulgarian National Bank may also initiate bankruptcy proceedings against insolvent banks. The Act also included specific regulatory provisions, such as:

- A bank may not, save by permission of the central bank, acquire shares, interest or other participation in a non-financial undertaking for a value exceeding 10 per cent of the capital of the undertaking.

- The amount of any bank's own capital shall be equivalent to at least 8 per cent of the risk capital of the bank.

- Any bank shall set aside at least one-fifth of its after-tax and pre-dividend profit in a rescue fund until the assets in the said fund reach 1.25 per cent of the total balance sheet amount of assets and guarantees and other securities assumed by the bank.

- No loan, credit concession or guarantee to an amount exceeding 15 per cent of the bank's own capital shall be offered to one person or to economically associated persons ('major loan'), save by a decision of the persons managing and representing the bank.

- No major loan offered by a bank or a group of banks may exceed 25 per cent of the bank's own capital.

- The total amount of major loans made shall be limited to eight times the amount of the bank's own capital.

CURRENT SITUATION AND OUTLOOK

The theory of full banking liberalisation in Bulgaria has yet to match practice. Many commercial banks still owe their existence to the funding requirements of certain industrial sectors. As a result, Bulgarian banks are often owned by the industries they service, which in turn have a decisive influence over their lending policies.

For example, First East Bank operates mainly within its original mandate of supporting the chemical industry, and allocates the majority of its total available credit lines to a few large individual chemical companies. Biochem Bank is principally involved in tourism projects on the Black Sea as a result of having among its shareholders around 85 companies, most of which are in the tourism sector. Other examples include the Electronics Bank, of which 44 per cent is held by electronics companies, which in turn receive 40 per cent of the bank's loan portfolio.

Demand for credit in Bulgaria is far higher than the present system can service, and scarcity is particularly acute in the private sector. Credit available in the system is reported to be exclusively limited to short-term, trade-related funding, commercial credit with a maturity of 3 to 90 days, and 'productional' credit, linked to the lifetime of the production of industrial goods.

Another problem faced by the banking industry is the need for an expanded and more efficient payments system. Cash is the main method of payment for Bulgarian individuals, and most enterprises resort to transfer orders on their current accounts. Cheques and bills of exchange have yet to be developed.

In the near future, a major study on structural issues of the banking system is expected to provide a detailed programme of mergers, acquisitions and takeovers. The government's objective is to reduce the total number of 78 commercial banks to no more than 12 institutions with diversified portfolios. The Bank Consolidation Company, which will implement this project, was formed in March 1992, and the bank shares held by the Bulgarian National Bank and the Foreign Trade Bank were transferred to it. Shares held by other state agencies will be similarly transferred starting from the second half of 1992.

In August 1992, the creation of a new commercial bank, the Bank of Bulgarian Credit, was announced. The new bank was formed as a result of the merger of 22 commercial banks as part of measures aimed at privatising the banking industry. The next banking merger is expected to take place between Bulgaria's two largest banks, the Economic Bank and Mineral Bank. These two banks between them are expected to control over a third of Bulgarian banking business. It is expected that this package of measures will reduce fragmentation, considered as one of the major obstacles to an efficient and modern banking system.

12

Accounting Standards

Touche Ross

Since the on-set of the economic reforms, the Ministry of Finance has set about implementing a legislative and regulatory framework which will, as quickly as possible, bring the Bulgarian accounting system into line with international standards. All in all, good progress has been made:

- The Accountancy Act entered into force on 1 April 1991 and provides the basic framework to be followed by most Bulgarian enterprises when preparing their annual financial reports.

- The Ministry of Finance has prepared, and the Council of Ministers approved, a National Chart of Accounts which aims to promote a uniform approach to the organisation of accounting systems operated by enterprises within Bulgaria.

- Tangible steps have been taken to establish an accounting profession within Bulgaria, with the first wave of certified public accountants being recognised under the Accountancy Act in late-1991.

THE ACCOUNTANCY ACT

The Accountancy Act provides a broad framework for the Bulgarian accounting system. While the Act sets out certain broad requirements regarding, for example, types of accounting documentation, valuation methods, reporting deadlines and the preservation of accounting records, it grants wide powers to the Ministry of Finance to evolve and promulgate the National Chart of Accounts, accounting standards, basic accounting documents and accounting techniques. The Act also provides authority for the setting up of a National

Accounting Council to act as consultant to the Ministry of Finance with the participation of members of the profession, universities, the Union of Bulgarian Accountants, together with the state and private sectors of the national economy.

The annual financial statements of certain forms of commercial company recognised under Bulgarian company law (including private limited and public limited companies) must be audited each year by one or more certified public accountants appointed by the general meeting of the company. The Accountancy Act acknowledges this requirement (other than for certain small or non-profit-making enterprises which are not required to carry out double entry accounting) and provides that the Ministry of Finance must settle any disagreements between a certified public accountant and enterprise concerning the approval of an annual financial report.

The salient provisions of the Accountancy Act are summarised in the remainder of this chapter.

General provisions

Most enterprises (defined as any legal entity or individual engaged in a legitimate economic activity) must use double entry accounting. Certain non-profit enterprises and enterprises employing an average of less than 10 people annually and with assets amounting to less than 50 times the average annual wages of their employees, are free to use single entry bookkeeping.

Accounts must be kept in the Bulgarian language and currency. Furthermore, the essential details of transactions recorded on basic accounting documents originally in a foreign language must be translated into Bulgarian.

In an attempt to meet international accounting standards, the Accountancy Act embodies the following principles:

■ All transactions must have documentary support.

■ The accounts must recognise the concept of 'prudence' which essentially requires the reporting of the enterprise's actual financial results with emphasis on substance over form, the recognition in the current period of any reasonable risks, possible future losses and asset write-downs and that receivables and payables are not offset.

■ Separate accounting periods should be treated independently.

■ The opening balance sheet of an accounting period should

equal in every respect the closing balance sheet of the preceding period.

■ The enterprise must be treated as a going concern.

■ Cost and depreciation accounting techniques must be consistent.

The Accountancy Act recognises and approves the use of computerised accounting systems.

Annual compliance

The accounting period for all enterprises is the calendar year ended 31 December and the enterprise's annual financial report must be completed by 15 February in the following year. The annual financial report must be presented to the statistical authorities by 31 March. Furthermore, non-state enterprises must publish their balance sheet and statement of income and expenses (profit and loss statement) in a national daily newspaper by 30 April. This latter requirement appears to apply to all private enterprises, no matter what their size or degree of foreign ownership. State-owned enterprises must present their annual financial report to the Chamber of Accounting in lieu of the publication requirement.

Essentially an annual financial report will comprise a balance sheet and profit and loss statement. The report must also include notes containing information regarding the asset and liability valuation and depreciation policies, explanations why such policies may have changed from those applied in earlier periods and the financial position of the enterprise.

Special requirements regarding the content and form of the annual financial reports of state budget-subsidised, banking and insurance entities may be determined by the Ministry of Finance and the head of the national statistical authority.

The Accountancy Act also recognises the concept of consolidated accounting and requires that an enterprise owning more than half of the shares of or voting power in another enterprise or controlling more than half of the membership of the board of directors of that enterprise must, in addition to its own financial report, prepare a consolidated report for the economic group by 15 March of the year following the accounting period in question. In addition, any enterprise owning shares in another enterprise must present its financial report to the statistical authorities by 15 March (and not 31

March as required in the case of other enterprises not preparing consolidated accounts).

An enterprise is required to retain its accounting records for a minimum of three years with special requirements applying to payroll information (50 years), accounting ledgers and statements (10 years) and finance and tax audit documents (until the next audit). Computerised accounting information must be stored on a magnetic storage device or microfilm under proper storage conditions for the same periods as described earlier.

Valuation and depreciation methods

Assets are sub-divided into non-current and current assets. Non-current assets are in turn sub-divided into tangible, intangible and financial assets, while current assets are sub-divided into inventories, receivables, financial assets and deferred expenses.

Assets may be valued at their acquisition cost, production cost or realisable value, at the discretion of the enterprise. Acquisition cost is represented by the aggregate cost of purchase and cost of conversion incurred in bringing the asset to its present location and condition. The production cost comprises the aggregate of the cost related to the production of an asset but does not include financial expenses, production and administrative overheads and extraordinary expenses.

Realisable value is the estimated selling price of the asset. Assets acquired through an exchange or barter transaction are evaluated by the realisable value of the exchanged assets.

Intangible non-current assets include incorporation and expansion costs, R&D products, software, patents, licences, concessions, know-how, trademarks and goodwill; these must be included in the balance sheet only where there is reasonable evidence of future economic benefits and an estimated value under one of the bases discussed earlier.

Inventories, including materials, spare parts, livestock, products, merchandise and work in progress, may be valued under one of four different bases: first-in-first-out (FIFO), last-in-first-out (LIFO), weighted average cost, and specific identification of inventory items. Inventories held at the year-end should be valued at the lower of their realisable or book value at the balance sheet date.

Foreign currencies held or receivable at the year-end must be evaluated at the closing rate of the Bulgarian National Bank if this value is lower than the amount previously recorded, and any difference must be charged as a financial expense. Similarly, securities, other than state securities, should be valued at the year-end at their realisable value, if this value is lower than the amount previously recorded. Again the difference should be charged as a financial expense. State securities should always be valued at par irrespective of their acquisition cost.

Enterprises are required to depreciate their tangible and intangible non-current assets, although no depreciation may be charged on land, forests and cultural monuments. An enterprise is entitled to establish its own depreciation norms depending on, in the case of tangible assets, their expected useful life and acquisition cost. In the case of intangible assets, the depreciation charge will depend on the actual investment and the period of amortisation, which should not exceed five years. The enterprise may choose the method of depreciation, be it straight-line or otherwise.

The Accountancy Act requires that the enterprise's assets and liabilities, other than tangible and intangible non-current assets, be subject to a stocktaking each year in connection with the preparation of the annual financial report. A stocktaking of the tangible and intangible non-current assets is required at least once every two years. Stocktakings are also required whenever ownership of the enterprise is changed.

The concept of accrued income and deferred expenses is recognised under the Accountancy Act. The income of an enterprise from the sale of goods, the provision of services and the use by third parties of the enterprise's resources (eg interest, royalties, rent and dividends) should be recognised in an accounting period unless a reasonable doubt exists as to whether the amount will be paid, in which case recognition of the income may be deferred.

On the other hand, expenses are to be recognised generally on an accruals basis regardless of the timing of their actual payment.

13

The Privatisation Process

Sinclair Roche & Temperley

Bulgaria is one of the last Eastern European countries to embark on a privatisation programme. Many consider it to be one of the region's higher risk and slower moving countries. Its industry has so far attracted little foreign interest because the lack of relevant legislation was taken as a lack of commitment to reform on the government's part. The Law on Transformation and Privatisation of State and Municipal Enterprises of 23 April 1992 (the 'Privatisation Law') now indicates a strong wish to alter the situation by promoting legal developments and 'kick-starting' Bulgarian industrial redevelopment.

Under the Privatisation Law, two lists have been published. One of large and the other of small enterprises with good economic potential. Whether an enterprise is large or small depends on the value of its assets. Altogether, 206 enterprises are listed from both heavy and light industries, the food industry and trade. To be included in the lists, an enterprise must:

1. be either in a comparatively good financial condition or operate in a sector with good economic potential to attract investors;

2. be in a sector safe from state monopoly and be ecologically acceptable; and

3. not be threatened by claims for the restitution of property confiscated by the former communist regime.

OUTLINE OF THE LAW

There was much political controversy about the Privatisation Law. It is a compromise clearly in favour of the free market approach which supports the sale of assets direct to trade buyers. It was opposed by those who favour the social approach, whereby assets are sold by way of employee buy-outs and offers of shares to the public. Though the Privatisation Law was passed in April 1992, its implementation has been hindered by ongoing political struggles, but it has finally resulted in a sector-by-sector programme that resembles strikingly Poland's privatisation programme. The hope is that a sectoral approach makes it easier to define which enterprises are most suitable for privatisation and sale.

The Privatisation Law itself is merely a framework setting out how a state enterprise is transformed into a one-man commercial company and how the privatisation of state-owned interests in such companies is effected.

The Privatisation Agency ('PA')

The PA has been created to develop an annual programme and to prepare a realisation report to be presented by the Council of Ministers ('CM') to the National Assembly, which discusses it and adopts it simultaneously with the State Budget Law. Data about executed sales is to be published every month in the *State Gazette*.

The PA effects sales of interests in enterprises, the capital value of which is over Lev10 million ($500,000). From Lev200 million ($10,000,000) and above, an approval of the CM must follow a proposal from the PA. Smaller sales are effected by an authority appointed by the CM – for example municipal councils are authorised to sell interests in enterprises owned by the municipalities.

Transformed companies must be offered for sale within five years of their transformation. The appropriate privatisation authority must rule upon a privatisation proposal within one month of its submission and, if the proposal is rejected, good reasons for the rejection must be given. These provisions, together with the annual programme developed by the PA, will put pressure on the authorities to implement the Privatisation Law quickly and reasonably.

Transformation and owner's rights

The transformation of a state enterprise into a one-man company is carried out by the CM or its delegated body in respect of small enterprises (capital of less than Lev10 million) and, for larger enterprises (capital of Lev10 million and above), by the CM itself, having first taken into consideration the PA's views. It should be noted that restitution claims from owners of real property who have not already been compensated are to be lodged within two months after publication of the privatisation decision, before or after the transformation, and by June 1993 at the latest. Claims submitted within the time limit entitle the claimant (if successful) to receive a proportion of the shares or stocks of the company privatised. Claims not submitted within the time limit would (if successful) only entitle the claimant to compensation for the loss.

Sale of shares and stocks owned by the Bulgarian state

Shares and stocks must be offered within five years from the date of transformation by public auction, public tender or negotiation with potential buyers. Direct sale is possible only in the case of joint stock companies or shares, provided that they are sold by the PA.

The valuation of companies is undertaken by independent Bulgarian or foreign experts licensed by the PA. The valuation procedure will be subject to further legislation.

The issue of shares in privatised companies in exchange for existing debt is subject to permission from the PA, as are payments for shares by instalments. Workers and employees of the enterprise also have rights to purchase shares on its privatisation. During the period of three months after the opening of an offer, they may purchase up to 20 per cent of the shares for sale at half the offer price. Shares so purchased are non-voting for three years. The government is examining a system of loans which would allow employees to borrow at low rates of interest for the purchase of such shares.

Sale of enterprises and assets

In the case of state and municipal-owned enterprises valued at less than Lev10 million ($500,000) which have not been transformed into commercial companies, their 'independent parts' and the assets of liquidated enterprises may be sold on the basis of an independent foreign or Bulgarian valuation, by public auction or by tender. Auctions are to be held 30–60 days after the initial announcement of the offer. If there is only one bidder, he is entitled to buy only at a second auction held at least 15 days after the first. Foreigners may only take part if they have already registered an undertaking in Bulgaria or filed an application to so register.

Real property may be disposed of by:

1. a lease for a period of 25 years with a purchase option;

2. a management contract with a purchase or selling option;

3.   a sale by instalments with a reservation of title until completion; or

4.   a sale subject to conditions such as the preservation of the design of the property, the number of employees, a commitment to investment, or the attainment of business targets.

If they win the auction or tender, employees receive a reduction in price of up to 30 per cent and may be permitted to pay by instalments adjusted by the rate of inflation.

EMPLOYEE PARTICIPATION

Any investor in an Eastern European country should examine not only opportunities to make profits in the short term but also how the country involves employees and workers. The latter is crucial to good labour and social relations. However, it is not easy to integrate and motivate employees on the one hand and attract foreign investors on the other.

The Bulgarian government attempts to achieve this harmony by giving employees an opportunity to buy their own enterprise and, if they fail to do so in full, to buy a share of up to 20 per cent with preferential rights. For investors the attraction is that they act on otherwise equal terms in that the 80 per cent which is free of preferential rights represents, for the three years during which the 20 per cent has no voting rights, 100 per cent control over the enterprise. This period should be sufficient to make the basic decisions on how the enterprise is to be run. For the employees, it is a time when they can prove the economic potential of the enterprise and keep it an attractive investment for both investors and themselves.

FOREIGN OPPORTUNITIES

The Privatisation Law declares that all natural persons and legal entities can take equal part in the privatisation programme. Although Bulgarian citizens, and especially employees, enjoy preferential rights, and Bulgarian enterprises will certainly be preferred to foreign persons in practice, such equality of treatment is unusual in Eastern Europe.

The new Law, together with the vital interest of the state in the rapid improvement of its economic situation, will provide the international market with good investment opportunities in Bulgaria.

14

Property Law
Sinclair Roche & Temperley

Of prime importance in structuring many foreign investments in
Central and Eastern Europe generally is the law concerning
ownership of land. In Bulgaria, the question of land ownership has
been addressed in the new Constitution, the Law on Ownership and
Use of Agricultural Land of 1991 (the 'Agricultural Land Law'), three
Restitution Acts passed since 1991, the Privatisation Law of 1992 and
the Law on the Economic Activity of Foreign Persons and the
Protection of Foreign Investments of 1992 (the 'FIL'). This chapter is
intended to consider the effect of such legislation for foreign
investors and will address the position as regards both agricultural
and non-agricultural land.

RIGHTS OF PRIVATE OWNERSHIP

There are no longer any restrictions on ownership of immovable
property by Bulgarian nationals residing in Bulgaria or by Bulgarian
legal entities which are not controlled by foreign parties.

Land is acquired by notarial deed executed before and registered
with a notary in the area in which the property is situated. As a
condition precedent to any transfer, a vendor must prove title to
property before the notary which will provide, effectively, a
guaranteed and fully investigated title. Subject to satisfaction of
such condition precedent, any party may freely transfer property.

As with many other jurisdictions in Central and Eastern Europe, a
distinction must be made between rights of ownership in land and
rights in respect of buildings. So, for example, under Bulgarian law a
building built on land with the landowner's consent becomes owned
by the builder for as long as the land on which it is built remains in
the ownership of the landowner.

AGRICULTURAL LAND

Since 1944, the control of all agricultural land has rested with the state, acting either directly through state enterprises or through co-operative structures.

The Agricultural Land Law (as recently amended) has effected a transfer of ownership of all agricultural land back to the previous owners, provided that:

- any owner who does not use agricultural land for a period of three years will be required to pay a municipality tax assessed on the value of the average yield of a similar sized unit in the same geographic area;

- no household shall acquire (through the provisions of the Agricultural Land Law) more than 600 decares (200 in specific areas of intensive agricultural production) – although unrestricted subsequent acquisition is allowed;

- no person may own agricultural land unless residing permanently in Bulgaria; and

- the land must be used for agricultural purposes only.

Under the FIL, foreign states and companies and Bulgarian companies with a foreign participation exceeding 50 per cent may not own agricultural land but do have rights to use land subject to the terms of relevant regulatory legislation which is still to be introduced. Pending introduction of such legislation it is still not possible for such foreign entities to acquire any rights of ownership or use in respect of agricultural land.

As regards foreign nationals (and Bulgarian nationals residing permanently abroad), such individuals may acquire agricultural land by inheritance only. In such cases the relevant individual must effect a transfer to any one of the state, the municipality or a Bulgarian resident national or legal entity within three years of inheriting the property. Such persons are also restricted in the same manner as foreign states and companies and Bulgarian companies with a foreign participation exceeding 50 per cent.

NON-AGRICULTURAL LAND

In its transition from a command to a free market economy Bulgaria has made a clear statement of intent in its new Constitution (passed in July 1991) with the recognition of private property ownership rights.

Restitution

Since 1991 the Bulgarian parliament has adopted three Restitution Acts affecting private ownership of immovable property. This legislation has effected a transfer back to previous owners or their heirs. However, problems have arisen in practice:

- in providing documentary evidence in support of any claim;
- in tracing previous owners; and
- in effecting restitution in the absence of detailed regulatory provisions for such purposes.

The Privatisation Law also provides for previous owners of property (constituting assets of state-owned companies and municipal enterprises) to acquire shares in the privatised companies on preferential terms (see Chapter 13). Similar rights exist in respect of claims over land in respect of which the state has acquired an interest through building of state or municipal enterprises. However, in cases where the previous owner has received financial compensation in respect of property, he has no right to participate in the capital of an enterprise on privatisation.

Restrictions on foreign ownership

In respect of non-agricultural land, restrictions on foreign ownership are contained within the FIL. Although foreign persons may acquire ownership rights in respect of buildings and may acquire other limited rights in respect of immovable property (eg a right to construct buildings), foreign persons may not acquire ownership rights in respect of land (either directly or indirectly) save where property is situated in particular geographical regions and consent is given by the Council of Ministers.

Direct ownership restrictions preclude ownership by foreign nationals residing permanently abroad, or by a foreign legal entity abroad. It is, however, possible for a Bulgarian company owned or controlled by a foreign person to own non-agricultural land in Bulgaria.

LEASING RIGHTS

Prior to the adoption of the FIL, it was possible to enter into long-term leases in respect of land (pursuant to Decree 56 on Economic Activities and previous foreign investment legislation). Since the 1992 legislation, leasing is regulated by the Law on Obligations and Contracts. This Law restricts the term of any lease to a maximum of 10 years, thus effectively restricting the opportunity for foreign investors to enter into long-term leases in respect of land. Any lease of land entered into under the previous legislation is unaffected by the new restrictions and will continue for the previously negotiated term, even if in excess of 10 years. No similar limits apply to leases of buildings (as distinct from the land on which they are built).

15

The Fiscal Framework

Touche Ross

The Bulgarian tax system is undergoing fundamental changes with many of the current laws merely acting as stop-gaps until the introduction of a comprehensive tax legislation package which will become operational from 1 January 1993. Principal elements of the package will include a revised profits tax law, a comprehensive personal income tax law and a value added tax (VAT) law.

Unfortunately details of the proposed tax changes have not yet been made available; however, according to the Bulgarian business press, the IMF, the World Bank and other international experts have recommended that the present tax concessions be minimised so as to avoid unfair competition between non-resident and domestic investors as well as private and state-owned companies.

While developing the tax package, the Ministry of Finance has also been busy setting up a tax administration with responsibility for collecting taxes, reviewing tax returns and so on. There are already at least 27 district offices with many more local offices located around the country. Tax offices will deal not only with the collection of profits tax and individual income tax but also turnover tax (and later VAT) and other taxes including property tax and car tax.

Recently published figures indicate that the government expects to raise some Lev40 billion (about US$1.7 billion) in taxes during 1992. The largest anticipated revenue earner is the profits tax (an estimated Lev22 billion) followed by excise duty (Lev8.3 billion) and turnover tax (Lev6.5 billion). Income tax is anticipated to raise some Lev2 billion.

Following a description of the tax incentives currently available to foreign investors, this chapter covers the principal taxes levied on business entities and individuals including:

- profits tax on business enterprises;

- income tax on individuals;

- turnover tax and excise duty.

Other taxes such as social insurance contributions, real estate tax and inheritance and gift tax are then covered in brief.

TAX INCENTIVES FOR FOREIGN INVESTMENT

The principal tax incentives available under Bulgarian law involve preferential profits tax rates and, in some cases, profits tax holidays, exemption from indirect taxes and the availability of free trade zones for use by both Bulgarian and foreign investors.

Profits tax concessions

Bulgarian incorporated companies with foreign participation in excess of 49 per cent and having a minimum share capital of US$100,000 (or an equivalent amount in another hard currency) receive preferential profits tax treatment. Such companies are taxed at the rate of 30 per cent while, until recently, the profits of companies with lower foreign participation were taxed at the higher rate of 40 per cent.

On 15 July 1992, the National Assembly adopted an amending Act extending the preferential 30 per cent rate to all private companies with annual taxable profits not in excess of Lev1 million, regardless of whether these companies are Bulgarian or foreign owned. However such companies may still remain subject to municipality tax which is levied at 10 per cent on taxable profits as well as a 2 per cent land improvement fund levy based on accounting profits (resulting in an effective tax rate of just over 40 per cent). Foreign-owned companies which are eligible for the 30 per cent rate as discussed above are not subject to the municipality tax but only the land improvement fund levy.

The profits derived by a branch of a non-resident company operating in Bulgaria are taxed at the normal rate of 40 per cent plus municipality tax and land improvement fund levy. The less attractive tax treatment of branches compared with locally incorporated subsidiaries of non-resident companies could give valid grounds for a claim in the case of a UK resident company under the non-discrimination article of the UK/Bulgarian double taxation convention.

A five-year profits tax holiday is available for companies in which there is a foreign participation in respect of business activities in certain priority sectors such as high technology, agriculture or food industries, as determined by the Council of Ministers. A three-year tax holiday was recently introduced for companies without state participation which carry out manufacturing activities. This holiday is available retrospectively from 1 January 1992 or from the date of registration of the company, if later.

Indirect tax concessions

Capital goods and raw material imports by foreigners for the production of goods for export are exempt from import duties as well as turnover tax or excise duties.

Free trade zones

Free trade zones have been established at Rousse, Bourgas, Vidin, Plovdiv, Svilengrad and Dragoman. Details of each of these free trade zones are contained in the Appendix to this chapter.

The basic aim of the free trade zones is to encourage productive, commercial and other export-orientated economic activities by Bulgarian or foreign investors. The import and export of goods and services to and from free trade zones are exempt from any customs or excise duty or turnover tax. This exemption also applies to any exchange of goods or services between the free trade zones; however, on 'importing' goods or services into Bulgaria from a free trade zone, customs duty and other indirect taxes will apply. Any goods located in the zones are subject to customs supervision.

The profits from productive, commercial and other economic activities carried on within the free trade zones are exempt from profits tax for a period of 5 years and will thereafter be taxed at 20 per cent. However, the profit from the sale of goods and the provision of services from the free trade zones into Bulgaria or abroad will be subject to taxation at 30 per cent (where the profit is remitted abroad) and 20 per cent (where the profit is invested in economic activities within the zone or in Bulgarian joint ventures).

A wide range of activities is permitted within the free trade zones, making the use of free trade zones a very attractive option for foreign investors.

PROFITS TAX

All forms of commercial company recognised under Bulgarian law will be subject to profits tax. As discussed earlier, the basic rate of profits tax is currently 40 per cent in the case of companies with taxable profits in excess of Lev1 million. Commercial banks are subject to the higher rate of 50 per cent. In addition there is a further municipality tax of 10 per cent on taxable profits and a land improvement fund levy of 2 per cent on the entity's accounting profits.

Bulgarian resident companies (those with their head office in Bulgaria) are subject to profits tax on their world-wide income under Bulgarian domestic law.

Under the double taxation convention between the UK and Bulgaria, the business profits of a UK enterprise earned from a business in Bulgaria will generally be taxable only in the UK unless the Bulgarian business is carried on through a 'permanent establishment'. A permanent establishment will be any fixed place of business in Bulgaria through which the enterprise wholly or partly carries on its business and will specifically include a place of management, branch, factory or workshop. In such a case, only the profits which are attributable to the Bulgarian permanent establishment will be taxable in Bulgaria.

A permanent establishment will be free to repatriate its profits to its head office overseas and it appears that under present law no further tax will be imposed in Bulgaria at this time.

Determination of taxable profits

A company's taxable profits are generally determined by adjusting accounting profits for the fiscal year, usually the 12-month period corresponding with the calendar year. For example, entertaining and business travel expenses incurred beyond a fixed amount set by the Ministry of Finance are non-deductible and must be added back to accounting profit. In a similar fashion, certain penalties incurred by the company, for example under environmental law or for breaching price control laws, must be added back.

Inter-company dividends received and profits of foreign-based branches of Bulgarian resident companies are exempt from profits tax. In the latter case, there is a condition that the profit was subject to tax in the country in which the branch is situated. Also tax-free is any interest earned by the company on government bonds.

Losses incurred in any fiscal year may be carried forward and deducted against profits for a period of up to five years. Other items which are specifically deductible in calculating taxable profits are:

- Voluntary contributions to certain social security funds which do not exceed 10 per cent of the gross annual profit of the company.

- Amortisation in respect of certain investment credits, or in the case of private companies, all investment credits.

- Interest expenses up to a ceiling of 25 per cent of the principal, or in the case of private companies, all interest expenses.

- Certain items of social expenditure such as medical care, business training and transport expenditure up to a ceiling of 10 per cent of the company's wage fund.

- All expenses incurred for investment purposes, excluding investments in shares and securities.

Tax depreciation is permitted, although the rules are quite complex and do not fall within the scope of this chapter.

Payment

Profits tax is paid in advance on a quarterly self-assessed basis. A similar payment scheme applies to the municipal tax, and late payment of tax due may incur very high levels of interest.

A final tax return must be submitted within 30 days from the date on which the company's annual financial statements have been approved by a recognised certified accountant or auditor, but not later than 31 March of the following fiscal year.

Withholding taxes

Payments received by non-residents in the form of dividends, interest, patent and copyright royalties and technical service charges are subject to withholding tax at a rate of 15 per cent. Joint stock companies with any foreign participation which receive dividends are taxed at the rate of 10 per cent of the gross dividend. There are indications that both of these rates may be increased to 20 per cent in the near future.

Withholding tax must be remitted to the fiscal authorities within 10 days of payment. However, dividends which are received by non-residents and are reinvested in purchasing shares or bonds within Bulgaria will be exempt.

It should be noted that the UK/Bulgaria double tax convention limits the withholding tax on dividends paid by Bulgarian resident companies to UK residents to 10 per cent, while interest and royalty withholding taxes are reduced to zero. Requests for refund of withholding taxes paid in excess of the treaty rate must be made to the tax authorities within a year of collection.

Taxation of UK resident companies

A UK resident company should not be subject to profits tax merely because it has a representative office, provided it does not carry on any business but limits its activities to, for example, the storage of goods for display, the purchase of goods, advertising, the collection and supply of information, or scientific research.

If, as stated above, the UK company maintains a fixed place of business or branch in Bulgaria through which it actively carries on business, any profits attributable to the branch will be subject to the Bulgarian tax regime.

TAXES ON INDIVIDUALS

Income earned by employed and self-employed individuals is subject to income tax at prescribed rates. Public institutions, like individuals, are subject to income tax, but at a flat rate of 20 per cent. Income derived by farmers from agricultural activities will be exempt from income tax until February 1996.

Individuals who are not Bulgarian citizens will nevertheless generally be treated as being resident in Bulgaria for taxation purposes during any calendar year in which they are present in Bulgaria for more than half the year.

Certain categories of income are exempted from income tax including pensions, scholarships, child support bonuses, alimony and proceeds from insurance policies. Furthermore proceeds from the sale of shares and bonds falling short of their nominal value will be exempt from income tax.

Employees are subject to tax, withheld from their wages by their employer, based on a progressive monthly marginal income tax scale. The current progressive annual income tax rates for employees are set out in Table 15.1. Income derived by individuals who are self-employed or who carry on a business, and dividend income received by individuals, are also taxed at the rates in Table 15.1. Individuals carrying on a business are allowed to write-off from their taxable

Table 15.1 *Employee income tax rates*

Tax rate (%)	Band of annual income (leva)
0	0 – 9,000
20	9,001 – 12,000
24	12,001 – 36,000
28	36,001 – 72,000
32	72,001 – 120,000
36	120,001 – 240,000
40	240,001 – Over

income all indispensable costs of carrying out their normal business activities and certain other prescribed deductible expenses.

Income tax returns must be submitted by 15 February in the year following the year of assessment (which is the calendar year) and any outstanding tax liability must be paid in one instalment.

Non-resident individuals will be subject to income tax in the same way as Bulgarian nationals in relation to work completed in Bulgaria. The UK/Bulgaria double tax convention ensures that remuneration derived by a UK resident individual in respect of an employment exercised in Bulgaria will be taxable only in the UK provided that the individual is present in Bulgaria for a total period not exceeding 183 days in the fiscal year concerned, that the remuneration is paid by or on behalf of a non-Bulgarian resident employer, and the remuneration is not borne by a permanent establishment or a fixed base which the employer maintains in Bulgaria.

Other exemptions from Bulgarian income tax cover activities such as service aboard a ship, aircraft, railway or road vehicle and service as a press, radio or television reporter. Directors' fees earned by a UK resident in his capacity as a member of the management or supervisory board or of the board of directors of a Bulgarian resident company may be taxed in Bulgaria under the convention.

TURNOVER TAX

Turnover tax is currently imposed on the retail sale of both domestically produced and imported consumer goods and the provision of services within Bulgaria. The turnover tax regime operates alongside an excise duty regime. Where excise duty is imposed on a particular domestic or imported product, turnover tax will not apply.

The principal turnover tax rate is 22 per cent while a lower 10 per cent rate applies to particular items, such as:

- certain foodstuffs including flour, meat, dairy products, eggs, fish, fruit and vegetables and edible plant oils;

- baby and childcare products;

- certain medical, pharmaceutical and other related materials;

- house rentals and passenger transport services;

- school books and materials other than university text books.

Certain essential items such as basic bread, electricity, hard coal, central heating and devices for disabled persons are exempted from the tax.

The basis for calculation of turnover tax is the retail selling price of the goods or services and the tax is generally borne by the seller. The seller will normally increase the price of the relevant goods or services in order to receive a sufficient mark-up or profit. For example, if the seller would normally sell his goods for Lev100 he will attempt to charge Lev128, which, taking into account turnover tax at 22 per cent, will leave him with approximately Lev100 for the sale. Turnover tax is imposed only on the final retail sale in Bulgaria and does not apply to exports or to sales to industrial users inside Bulgaria.

As stated earlier, it is proposed that the turnover tax regime will be replaced by a VAT commencing on 1 January 1993. It is likely that there will be a single rate of VAT, perhaps 20 per cent. Although the VAT has, with the help of international experts, been drafted as closely as possible to the European Community model, it is likely that the law will be far less complex. It is also likely that the excise duty regime discussed below will continue to apply.

EXCISE DUTIES

As discussed earlier, excise duties are imposed on certain groups of luxury goods or goods considered detrimental to public health. Like the turnover tax, excise duties are levied on both domestic and imported goods and services falling within the various categories. Excise duty rates currently vary from between 10 per cent and 70 per cent although draft legislation has been prepared which would significantly lower and in some circumstances eliminate the present rates on particular items.

Some examples of rates are:

- alcoholic spirits, jewellery and precious metals – 70 per cent;

- perfumes, tobacco and cigarettes – 60 per cent;

- leatherwear and fur coats – 50 per cent;

- wine, beer, coffee, tea, video tape recorders, cassettes and compact discs, matches and gas lighters – 40 per cent;

- gasoline – 40 per cent;

- diesel – 25 per cent;

- propane – 10 per cent.

The draft excise duty legislation would decrease the duty on alcoholic beverages to 30 per cent, gasoline to 20 per cent and tape and video recorders, cassettes and compact discs to zero.

Like the turnover tax, excise duty will not apply to exports or sales to industrial users within Bulgaria.

OTHER TAXES

Social insurance contributions

Employers are required to make social insurance contributions in respect of each Bulgarian national employee to the National Social Insurance Department, generally at the rate of 35 per cent of the employee's gross wages (although the rate may be 45 per cent or 50 per cent depending on the relevant job category). These contributions are then paid into a fund which is held for the benefit of employees including the state pension, sickness, pregnancy and other benefits.

Employers must also make social insurance contributions in respect of foreign nationals employed in Bulgaria, at the rate of 20 per cent of the employee's gross monthly remuneration. They must also make contributions to the state unemployment fund, equal to 7 per cent of the total payroll.

Self-employed individuals must make social insurance contributions on their own account.

Real estate tax

An annual tax on buildings and real estate is levied on either the owner or the manager of the property. The tax is levied at rates of up to 6 per cent computed on an assessment of the value of the property made by the fiscal authorities. The rate which applies in relation to most private houses is 4 per cent, although additional tax may be levied where the floor area of the house exceeds 120 square metres.

Public gardens and facilities, sports centres, places of worship and land used for railway, air and water transport are exempt from the tax.

Inheritance and gift tax

Both Bulgarian and foreign citizens are liable to tax in relation to property located in Bulgaria which they have inherited or received as a gift. Certain types of property and legacies are exempt from the tax – otherwise the taxable amount is determined by the value of the property. Tax rates vary between 2 per cent and 50 per cent.

APPENDIX – FREE TRADE ZONES

1. **Rousse** – situated on the banks of the River Danube, close to the international motorway which runs along Danube Bridge. The zone was established in 1988 with an area of 800 hectares including 7000 square metres of warehouses and production facilities.
    Business contacts address:
    Svobodna Bezmitna Zona
    5 Kniajevska Street
    PO Box 108
    7000 Rousse
    Tel: (082) 72306
    Tlx: 62285 SBZ BG
    Fax: (082) 70084

2. **Bourgas** – located close to the Port of Bourgas. The zone was set up in 1989 and is still in the process of organisation. The zone is favourably located to several modes of transport including ship, air and motorway.
    Business contacts address:
    A F Svobodna Bezmitna Zona
    1 Toutrakan Street
    PO Box 154
    8000 Bourgas
    Tel: (056) 42858
    Tlx: 83316
    Fax: (056) 42047

3. **Vidin** – this zone has been under construction since 1988 on a new site next to a ferry terminal and a new cargo port on the Danube. There are 5000 square metres of newly built warehouses.
    Business contacts address:
    Svobodna Bezmitna Zona
    Vidin 3700
    Tel: (094) 22837, 22083
    Tlx: 36560
    Fax: (094) 30947

4. **Plovdiv** – this zone was incorporated in 1989 as a joint stock company. The zone occupies several compounds favourably located in the vicinity of the fairgrounds and in industrial areas in different parts of the city. The zone accommodates both warehouses and producers and open air storage area is available.
    Business contacts address:
    A F Svobodna Bezmitna Zona
    25 Veliko Turnovor Street
    4000 Plovdiv
    Tel: (032) 233462, 232503
    Fax: (032) 232503

5. **Svilengrad** – set up in late-1989 as a state company, with prospects to grow into a joint venture corporation. It is located close to the international motorway leading to Istanbul, at the junction of the Bulgarian, Greek and Turkish borders. Warehouses are already available for renting.
    Business contacts address:
    D F Svobodna Bezmitna Zona
    60 Bulgaria Boulevard
    6500 Svilengrad
    Tel: (0379) 2673, 6448
    Tlx: 43360
    Fax: (0379) 6479

6. **Dragoman** – established in 1991 on the territory of the Dragoman municipality which borders on Yugoslavia.
    Business contacts address:
    Dragoman Municipal Council
    2210 Dragoman
    Tel: 997172/2014

16

Communications
Touche Ross

The transition to a market economy and improved economic relations with the outside world have necessitated the swift development of the Bulgarian communications system. Capital expenditure on communications amounted to Lev2.2 billion in 1989, having more than doubled during the 1980s.

TELEPHONE, TELEX AND POSTAL SERVICES

There are currently over 2.3 million direct telephone exchange lines (DELS) in the country and there were over 2.5 million telephone units installed in 1989, of which 1.6 million were home telephones. However, telex communications are considered to be unsatisfactory – the number of telexes amounted to only 7400 units in 1989. The number of telex terminals is not expected to increase significantly and may even fall when facsimile transmission is made more reliable by network improvements.

Bulgaria's telegraph and telephone network is highly automated. Nevertheless, its telecommunications lag behind West European standards. Although telephone production rose to 1.192 million units in 1989, domestic demand has not been met. There is a large waiting list for residential and business lines – some estimates assess the waiting time as at least six years.

The data available regarding telephone sets and the density of telephone services indicates that there is a significant but very varied demand for telecommunication products. Perhaps surprisingly, Bulgaria has one of the highest telephone densities in Eastern Europe.

Bulgaria's telecommunications equipment production will in future

Table 16.1   *Tariffs for postal, telegraph and telephone services as of 1 May 1992 (inland)*

Item	Charge (leva)
Local letter up to 50g	1.0
For every next 50g or part thereof	0.3
Postal wrappers and small parcels	1.0
For every next 50g or part thereof	0.3
Registered letters	1.0
Express letters	1.0
Parcel post (1 district/different districts)	
Weight up to 3kg	5.5/6.40
Weight from 3 to 5kg	6.9/8.70
Weight from 5 to 7kg	8.5/11.1
Weight from 7 to 10kg	11.3/14.5
Weight from 10 to 12kg	12.4/16.8
Weight from 12 to 15kg	14.5/20.0*
Postal orders	
Up to Lev100	2.0
Lev101 up to Lev1000	
for every Lev100 or part thereof	1.0
More than Lev1000 or a part thereof	0.5
Telegrams	
Ordinary up to 20 words	2.0
For every word over 20	0.5
Express telegrams – double the ordinary rate	
Express ('flash') telegrams – triple the ordinary rate	

* For parcels more than 15kg and up to 20kg–Lev0.5 for every next kg.

be oriented towards new technologies through entering into co-operation agreements with major European and world producers. Demand in the next few years will be determined by the transition to digital telecommunication systems, commutation equipment, telephone sets and complementary telephone services. The biggest development in the sector in the near future will be the implementation of a digital overlay network which will act as the country's telecommunications backbone and should stimulate growth. The estimated cost of the digital overlay network is $150 million and it is being financed by various development banks.

ROADS

The location of Bulgaria in the central part of the Balkan Peninsula has had a positive influence on the development of its transport

network and should continue to do so. The country is close to the
'bridge' between Europe, Asia and Africa and is situated on both the
Black Sea and the River Danube. The total length of Bulgarian roads
in 1989 was some 36,935 kilometres or 33.2 kilometres per 100
square kilometres. Of these only 266 kilometres are highways and
2935 kilometres first-class roads.

Bulgaria is crossed by several important international roads (the
so-called E-roads) which are a part of the European road network.
The total length of these roads is 2500 kilometres.

Road transport plays an important role in the shipment of goods. In
1989, for example, it accounted for 71 per cent (312 million tons) of
the total volume of goods traffic.

RAILWAYS

Bulgaria has a well-developed rail network which presently consists
of 6597 kilometres of track, or 5.9 kilometres per 100 square
kilometres. The rail network has three major axes: the North
Bulgarian; the South Bulgarian; and the Sub-Balkan railway lines.

The ferryboat line Varna-Ilichevsk (OND) has increased the
importance of the North Bulgarian railway since a great volume of
goods are transported through the port of Varna to and from the
former USSR.

SEA

Sea transport plays a vital part in the economy of Bulgaria and a key
role in foreign trade. The Danube is the only river within the country
that can be used for the transportation of goods. It links Bulgaria with
most Central and West European countries.

Major seaports are located at Varna and Bourgas. Some 30–34
million tons of goods are handled annually in the Bulgarian ports:
Varna (nearly 10 million tons) and Bourgas (nearly 20 million tons).
There is also a container terminal in the port of Varna-Zapad which is
equipped to store up to 1000 international standard-size containers.

The Bulgarian merchant fleet runs up to 100 sea vessels (of which
12 are tankers) with a total loading capacity of 1.81 million tons
deadweight. Most of the vessels are 5 to 19 years old. The merchant
fleet maintains 10 regular lines, including 4 lines for the transportation of crude oil and oil products. A container line between the Varna
and Cuban ports is also in operation.

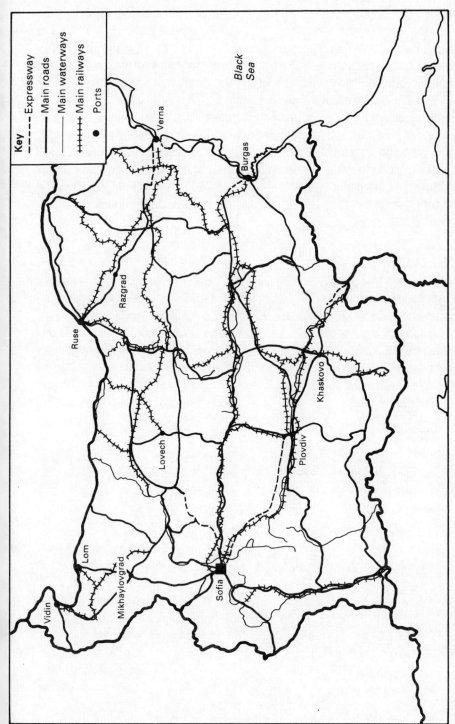

Map 16.1 *Infrastructure in Bulgaria*

AIR

Bulgaria's principal airport is located in Sofia. The Bulgarian airline, BALKAN, possesses some modern aircraft and offers direct and regular connections with a number of countries. Apart from Sofia, there are international airports in Varna, Bourgas and Plovdiv. Domestic services are operated from Sofia to Vidin, Varna, Bourgas, Rousse, Tirgoviste, Silistra, Haskovo and Gorna Oryahovitsa.

A new international airport is to be built on terrain recommended by IATA, not far from Sofia. The construction period of the airport complex is envisaged to be 3.5–5 years. The new airport is intended to meet all international standards for an international airport falling within category 3.

PRIORITIES

Priorities for the development of the transport infrastructure include, first, the Trans-European road, Kalotina-Kapitan Andreevo (E-80), with financing provided by the successful tender party and construction taking from 3–5 years. A joint exploitation is envisaged over a 20–30 year period following which ownership will transfer to the Bulgarian party.

The second priority is the Vidin–Sofia–Kulata road (E-79) resulting from the forthcoming operation of the Rhine–Main–Danube Channel and the accompanying interest of European Community countries in general.

Last but not least, Iran is interested in the development of the Bulgarian Danube ports as well as the Black Sea ports of Varna and Bourgas for the construction of reloading terminals.

17

The Environment

Touche Ross and Sinclair Roche
& Temperley

CURRENT STATE

As was the case in other Central and Eastern European countries, environmental deterioration in Bulgaria was a result of the command and control economy, utopian overestimation of heavy industry as a 'producer of the proletariat', non-market pricing of energy and raw materials, over-industrialisation and outdated technology usage.

Because of the geographical features of the country, there is little sense in using average data for Bulgaria as a whole. It is more realistic to speak about the various environmental 'hot spots'.

Despite high pollution levels, there are a variety of relatively clean areas with good conditions for agriculture – for example north-central and south-west Bulgaria. However, Bulgaria ranks before Poland and Hungary in sulphur dioxide pollution. This causes significant health problems in the hot spots. The same is the case with blood-lead levels in two south Bulgarian cities (Asenovgran and Kurdgaly) – the highest in international comparison.

Air

Estimated overall, Bulgarian emissions in 1989 were 1.7 million tons of sulphur dioxide, 0.3 million tons of nitrogen oxide, 0.15 million tons of hydrocarbons and 2 million tons of other pollutants. The power sector is the biggest polluter. There is almost no purifying equipment in the power plants. In some cases the concentration of sulphur dioxide in flue gases reaches 9000 milligrams per cubic metre (the EC standard is 400). Since 1991, there has been an additional significant sulphur polluter – the petrol refinery near

Bourgas (on the Black Sea shore). The reason for this is that Bulgarian crude oil imports were converted from Russian oil (one per cent sulphur content) to Middle East oil (six per cent).

Measured annually, the average concentrations of dust in all large Bulgarian cities is above the EC standard.

Water

All Bulgarian rivers are badly polluted with chemicals, heavy metals and sewage effluent. Towns with population of over 50,000 residents should have sewage systems, but only around one quarter of them are in any condition to operate efficiently. One-fifth of the sewage and industrial effluents of Sofia (over 1.2 million population) flowing into the Iskar river are not treated at all (there is a joke that using chemical analyses of Iskar water, one can learn the Mendeleev's Table).

Drinking water seems not to be a problem, with a few exceptions due to heavy metal radioactive contamination of the groundwater. Drinking water in three regions (Bourgas, Stara Zagora and Turgoviste) has ten-years concentration of nitrates above the standard. Not unusual are pollution cases due to technology mismanagement and decay; the best known case is probably the arsenic pollution of the river Topolnitza, having a standard of 50 micrograms per litre. Levels of 1440, 390 and 470 micrograms have been measured in pools up the river. In some water supplies near Topolnitza, arsenic levels were measured up to 286 micrograms and they have been closed for human usage.

Soil, forest and nature reserves

There are 11 million hectares of land in Bulgaria, 6.8 million of them set aside for agriculture and 3.9 million for forest. About 14 per cent of the land is eroded, nearly 90,000 hectares are affected by mining, and 46,000 hectares are contaminated by heavy metals. The problem is that heavy metal pollution comes from plants located right in the middle of the best agricultural regions, as is the case with the lead and zinc smelter near Plovdiv and the Kremikovtzi steel mill near Sofia. Reprivatisation in such areas can cause social tensions and significant health problems.

The average age of the Bulgarian forest reserves in 1990 was 42 years. There is no reliable data on forest deterioration. The total protected area is 200,000 hectares with 10 national reserves, 28 botanical reserves and 17 biosphere reserves. A newly drafted Protected Areas Law has been submitted recently to the parliament.

Environmental policy and public awareness

Environmental awareness has played a crucial role in Bulgarian social change since the mid-1980s. But, in general, environmental concerns were simply a form of public protest. As a result, the public is worried, but not active. There is a distinct lack of the practice to pursue one's own rights, and there is no consistent government environmental policy.

Nevertheless, Bulgaria differs from the rest of the countries of the region, having a very comprehensive Environmental Protection Law (EPL) adopted in October 1991. It establishes access to information, public participation, environmental impact assessment (EIA), and determines the duties of the local and national governments. It also contains lists of projects subject to compulsory EIA. In such cases, the investor should apply for a permit from the local municipality if the project is likely to affect the environment of one community, from the Regional Environmental Inspectorate (the local body of the Ministry of Environment) in case the project will affect territory of more than one community, and from the Ministry if the project will affect the territory of more than one Inspectorate. The mediator in the first two cases should be the local government body.

Energy

Bulgaria is characterised by very modest energy resources. In fact the country disposes of 8 times less than the world average and has almost 50 times less than the average reserves of the East European countries (former members of Comecon). Indicative in this respect is the fact that the local resources of high quality organic fuels (bituminous coal, crude oil and natural gas) provide less than one per cent of the total needs of the country. The serious problems in the power supply of Bulgaria can be seen from the structure of its energy balance (see Table 17.1).

The modest national energy resources of Bulgaria can also be seen in a synthetised form from the role of the net import in the visible consumption of primary energy and primary energy resources which is: primary energy – 68 per cent; liquid fuel – 98 per cent; natural gas – 96 per cent; solid fuel – 26 per cent; electric energy – 9 per cent.

The problem in Bulgaria is also critically complicated by

Table 17.1   *Structure of the energy balance in Bulgaria (in %)*

	Production	Consumption
1. Primary energy total	100	100
2. Solid fuel	88	46
3. Liquid fuel	2	35
4. Natural gas	1	15
5. Electric energy	9	4

comparatively low energy effectiveness. For example, energy use as a part of the GDP of Bulgaria is 2.3 times higher than in Japan, 2.36 times higher than in Germany and 1.45 times than in the USA (use of energy in GDP measured in kilogrammes arbitrary fuel per US1 dollar).

Energy use is a major factor for ecological imbalance, especially in respect of atomic energy, which produces about 40 per cent of total electric production in Bulgaria. The main problem is that the reactors of Kozlodui atomic station are physically and morally (mostly morally) antiquated. This is true of the whole material and technical basis of the Bulgarian energy industry, but the problem is most urgent for atomic energy. In fact the Bulgarian atomic energy industry is at the moment in a state of collapse.

At present in Kozlodui, only one block out of five functions, producing 220 megawatts. The remaining blocks are under reconstruction and repair. One is expected to be put back on line in November 1992 while the others may not be put back on line at all, or will be on line as late as August 1993. Evidently part of the foreseen ECU11.5 million from the PHARE program for the safety of atomic stations in Eastern European countries should go to Bulgaria, where the energy balance is the most dependent on the production of atomic energy.

The main problem in this field is the lack of absolute safety and reliability in the functioning of the atomic reactors. On the other hand, the cut back in capacities in Kozlodui will require enormous new investment, mostly foreign investment, in order to cover the total energy consumption of the country. According to official government data, if only blocks five and six of Kozlodui are stopped, it will be necessary to import energy from the Ukraine and Poland costing about $10 million, which could be obtained only as humanitarian aid from the EC.

The energy problem in Bulgaria is also complicated (particularly in the field of atomic energy) by the low professional qualifications of the individuals employed in this field. According to official data (although of an approximate character), 100,000 people are employed in the energy sector, but only 23 per cent of them are highly qualified. Also indicative in this respect is the data for the period 1977–1986: in Kozlodui, EC breaches were observed through fault of the operating personnel or objective causes, both intensified by incompetent interference.

The synthesised picture of the present-day Bulgarian energy industry discussed above leads to three main conclusions:

1. the material and technical basis is out-of-date, physically and morally;

2. the modernisation of energy production will require substantial foreign investments – mainly from the EC, as well as great national efforts; and

3. Bulgaria could potentially become a good market for western investments in energy as well as an intermediary point for transnational investments in this field.

PRIORITIES FOR GOVERNMENT AND AID PROGRAMMES

Economic prerequisites

Since February 1991, hard budget constraints, a reduction of subsidies, lower real prices for raw materials and energy, and charges, fees and penalties required by the EPL for environmental resources usage and environmental damage, will positively affect environmental protection. A stabilising nominal interest rate was also established last year. It remains at 54 per cent. Several opportunities to reduce this rate were not taken for political reasons (trade union activities, general elections and so on). It is foreseeable that high interest rates will continue during 1992. As a result, the circulation of capital will be restricted to the small trade business, small and medium-sized enterprises in the light industry sector and agricultural bodies with well negotiated external markets. However, long-term environmental and energy projects will lack domestic financial resources. Foreign investors with external funding for use by Bulgarian joint ventures may favour such projects.

Programme areas

It is possible that the economic restructuring will be a part of the privatisation programme. However, because of a lack of resources, the national government has not yet defined an environmental programme. It will concentrate on legislative work, the first priority being to identify environmental priorities.

Bearing in mind the above, it is possible to isolate the following areas as targets for aid programmes:

■ consultant activities in environmental auditing, risk technology assessment, and market incentives implementation;

■ funding activities in relatively clean regions, especially in agriculture and tourism, and light industry and high technology in the rest of the country;

■ investing in recycling and cleaning activities, waste treatment (there are some indirect taxation incentives for such investments), separation of wastes and even simple recycling are almost unknown as a field of real business activity;

■ monitoring and data management systems; and

■ EIA training and education of personnel and the public.

ENVIRONMENTAL LAW

The principal Bulgarian legislation on the protection of the environment is Law 326 on the Environment adopted on 2 October 1991 (the 'Environment Act'). The Act deals with environmental regulations and liability as well as the creation of environmental administrative bodies.

Environmental regulations

The corner-stone of the Environment Act is the prevention of risk to the environment and public health by the application of the 'best accessible technologies ... methods ... and international practices'. An important feature of the Act is the creation of a licensing system whereby those discharging pollutants into the environment must pay a fee to obtain a licence to carry out such activities.

The Environment Act also prohibits the import of dangerous substances or waste for disposal in Bulgaria. Significantly, this prohibition also extends to the importation of technologies harmful to the environment and the building or operation of plants without the necessary treatment facilities.

Perhaps the most significant regulations in the Environment Act are those in respect of environmental impact assessments, which closely resemble existing EC environmental legislation. However, the Act provides that such assessments apply not only to prospective activities but also, in certain circumstances, to existing activities. Thus, the Environment Act could be seen as creating a statutory obligation to undertake environmental audits. A list of categories of activities is specified in respect of which mandatory assessments must be conducted when a project has been proposed or existing activities are expanded. Briefly, these include infrastructure projects, petrochemical, iron/steel, metal processing and electronic plants as well as certain agricultural/forestry activities. However, it should be remembered that the Bulgarian environmental authorities retain a discretionary power to order assessments for *any project* which could have a significant impact on the environment. The Act specifies in some detail the procedures to be applied when conducting assessments: parties who can make representations, publication of information as well as the decision-making and appeal procedures. The foreign investor should particularly note that the business or project proposer is responsible for the cost of the assessment which in some cases could be quite significant.

Freedom of access to environmental information

The Environment Act places a duty on all persons engaged in the production of goods or the provision of services to submit to the Minister of the Environment certain environmental information concerning their business. This information is then freely available for inspection. A person failing to provide the requisite information can be ordered to do so by the Bulgarian courts. The significance of these provisions should not be underestimated as the freedom of access to information will inevitably lead to pressure for the enforcement of environmental regulations and liability of enterprises failing to comply with them.

Regulatory authorities

The Environment Act creates a three-tier system of regulatory authorities. The first tier is the Minister of the Environment who is responsible for licensing, the formulation of environmental quality standards and the conduct and monitoring of environmental impact assessments.

The second tier is the Regional Environmental Inspectorate which is appointed by the Minister of the Environment and to whom administrative functions are delegated.

The third tier is the relevant township which is responsible for developing local environmental protection plans and the control of domestic waste disposal.

Environmental liabilities

The Environment Act adopts the fundamental principle that the polluter pays and, accordingly, a party which has suffered loss/ damage as a result of pollution is entitled to compensation and/or the polluter may additionally be required to carry out restorative actions.

Where an environmental impact assessment has been carried out and it is determined that an activity is harmful to the environment or that the activity does not have the necessary waste treatment facilities, then the Minister for the Environment or the Regional Inspectorate has the power to order that the activity be discontinued, either temporarily or permanently. Failure to comply with such an order can result in fines or imprisonment. Similarly, a person who has failed to carry out an environmental impact assessment where such an assessment is mandatory may also be subject to a 'stop' order.

Fines for breaches of the environmental regulations under the Act range from the equivalent of US$250–125,000 for non-criminal breaches by businesses, up to the equivalent of US$1000–100,000 for breaches of stop orders or where it can be shown that irreparable harm has been caused to the environment. Terms of imprisonment up to a maximum of five years may be imposed where a person has continued with construction work in breach of an order prohibiting such work.

Conclusion

It will be seen from the above that the environmental regulations and liabilities provided for by the Environment Act are detailed and significant. For the present, the enforcement of these provisions may be piecemeal, but a foreign investor ignores the potentially stringent effects of environmental liabilities at his/her peril. The foreign investor should especially beware of finding him/herself in the position where it acquires a Bulgarian business and assumes the liability for past environmental damage caused by that business or its previous owner.

18

The Labour Market

Touche Ross and Sinclair Roche
& Temperley

In 1989, the number of employees in all sectors of the Bulgarian economy amounted to some 3.9 million. The share of women in the total was almost 50 per cent – about 1.9 million. The latter fact reflects in large part the non-sex discrimination policies applied in the former socialist society.

The political and economic changes underway in Bulgaria since 1989 have caused serious alterations in the structure and mobility of the labour force. More than 300,000 Bulgarian citizens have emigrated, mostly higher education graduates. In September 1991, 343,345 people were registered in the national labour exchange bureau while, at the same time, the number of jobs offered was only 18,486.

Labour market developments are difficult to assess in the absence of reliable data on private sector activity. Official employment declined by about 800,000 in 1991, while measured unemployment increased by 400,000. The difference cannot be fully accounted for. About 50,000 persons seem to have gone into early retirement while another 100,000 have registered as private entrepreneurs. The remaining 250,000 probably went either into the informal sector or did not register as unemployed because they were not entitled to benefits. The increase in net unemployment obscures a high turnover – during 1991, 800,000 persons became unemployed of whom 400,000 were able to find new jobs during the year. This suggests quite substantial labour mobility.

Also in September 1991, the average number of public sector employees was 3.271 million. Of these, 1.219 million were engaged in industry, 0.575 million in agriculture, 0.205 million in transport, 0.220

million in construction, 0.45 million in communications and 0.18 million in forestry.

PAY RATES

In Bulgaria employees' wages are regulated by decrees issued by the Council of Ministers and the Central Council of Trade Unions, and individual contracts.

Basic pay may fall into one of the following categories: time rate (per hour, per day or monthly pay rates); or piece rate (per item), which is determined on the basis of internal rules, accepted in the enterprises. By Decree 129 of the Council of Ministers (12 July 1991), a new system of pay rates was introduced in Bulgaria. The Decree must be applied by all employers whether state owned or private. The new system of basic pay rates is being implemented through negotiation on different levels:

- on a national level – between the government and the representative national organisations including unions and employers;

- at enterprise level – between the employer and the representative organisations of the unions;

- at branch level – between the branch organisations of the unions and the employer; and

- at a district level – between the regional syndicates and the employers.

The basic pay rate as negotiated in the collective labour agreement serves as a basis for setting basic pay rates in individual labour agreements.

In accordance with the Decree of 1 July 1991, the minimum monthly pay rate has been set at Lev620 (soon to be raised to Lev850) and the minimum hourly pay rate at Lev3.44.

In budget-financed organisations the basic pay rate is calculated according to a list of 10 official levels. Each official level corresponds to a number of job titles and a coefficient is allocated to it. The basic pay rate is a result of multiplying the initial pay rate by the corresponding coefficients.

In February 1992, the average monthly wage of public sector employees was as set out in Table 18.1.

Table 18.1 *Monthly public sector pay (average)*

Sector	Rate (in leva)
Industry	1623
Construction	1513
Forestry	1157
Transport	1605
Communications	1396
Trade, distribution, supplies	1357
Other production sectors	1805
Public utilities and consumer services	1412
Science	1565
Education	1407
Culture and arts	1287
Health, social security, sports and tourism	1450
Finance, credit, insurance	2261
Administration	1544
Other non-production sectors	1689
Total average salary (excluding agriculture)	**1543**

The Ministry of Finance and the Ministry of Labour and Social Policy, in co-operation with the IMF, have prepared draft legislation for the regulation of wage levels in state-owned enterprises in 1992. Updated information will be issued each quarter. Upper growth limits have been determined on the basis of predicted price levels. For the first quarter of 1992, the limit was 113.92 per cent, for the second quarter 110.6 per cent, for the third quarter 108.2 per cent, and for the fourth quarter 106.6 per cent. In case the rate of inflation exceeds the predicted levels, new negotiations are to be conducted between the government and the unions.

SOCIAL SECURITY SYSTEM

The social security system in Bulgaria provides for both short and long-term benefits for all workers and employees of the state, co-operative enterprises, joint ventures, private companies, for all employees of the Ministry of Defence, the Ministry of Interior Affairs and their respective departments.

The social security system is managed by National Social Insurance (NSI). Its funds are raised from employers' insurance contributions and independent insurance contributions by:

1. owners of private companies;

2. individual farmers;

3.   members of farmers' co-operatives;

4.   artisans;

5.   tenant farmers;

6.   individual commodity producers; and

7.   lawyers, artists and other self-employed professionals.

By Decree 43 of the Council of Ministers of 18 March 1991 social security contributions are determined as follows:

■   for persons who have the right to receive retirement pensions under the conditions of the III category of labour (discussed later) – 35 per cent of the nominal pay rate or declared income;

■   for persons who have the right to receive retirement pensions five years earlier than the age required for the III category of labour – 45 per cent of the nominal pay rate or declared income;

■   for persons who have the right to receive retirement pensions 10 and more years earlier than the age required for the III category of labour – 50 per cent of the nominal pay rate or declared income.

The contributions of independently employed individuals are deposited at their expense and are calculated as a percentage of declared income.

Short term benefits are paid as follows:

1.   in case of sickness;

2.   in case of work-related accident, illness or disease;

3.   maternity allowance paid during periods of maternity leave and equal to 100 per cent of the employee's wage but not less than the national minimum salary;

4.   child-birth benefit;

5.   child-care period benefit;

6.   family care allowance;

7.   monthly additions to one of the parent's wages for each child;

8.   salary differentials paid if employees are forced to accept another job at a lower salary due to their state of health.

Special regulations for social assistance operate under Decree 46 of the Council of Ministers of 25 March 1991. These regulations impose conditions under which the local government bodies (city councils) will support all people requiring social assistance. For this purpose monthly, periodical and one-off social benefits and other services will be granted. According to the regulations, each person or family member may be supported by a monthly benefit, the amount of which when added to the monthly income should provide for 65 per cent of the national minimum pay rate.

The local government bodies responsible for social security provide different forms of assistance including:

- free food in social security catering establishments;
- free transport tickets once a year for mothers of more than two children (including rail, road and water transport within the country);
- deliveries of foodstuffs, clothes and other basic goods, paying public utility services, etc;
- free season tickets for disabled persons; and
- free or subsidised medicines.

The local government bodies together with firms, foundations and charity organisations may also sell or freely distribute foodstuffs, clothes and other humanitarian aid for the poor.

Long-term benefits include retirement pensions, disability pensions, and dependant and spouse pensions.

Retirement pensions are received by all employees, workers, farmers, lawyers, artists, etc according to categories determined by the Council of Ministers:

- I category – 15 years of service and aged 50 for men and 45 for women;
- II category – 20 years of service and aged 55 for men and 50 for women;
- III category – 25 years of service and aged 60 for men and 55 for women.

Female employees who have given birth to 5 or more children up to the age of 8 may receive a retirement pension for 15 years of service and at the age of 40 for the I category of labour and at the age of 45 for II and III categories of labour.

Male teachers may receive a retirement pension for 25 years of service at the age of 55, while female teachers will qualify after 20 years' service at the age of 50.

In the event of the full or partial liquidation of an enterprise, redundant employees may receive a retirement pension where they have 25 years of service and are aged 57 for men or 20 years of service and aged 52 for women. These workers receive a 10 per cent decreased pension up to the usual retirement.

TRADE UNIONS

In addition to the three main trade unions (the Confederation of Independent Syndicates in Bulgaria, the Independent Labour Federation *Podkrepa* and the Syndicate *Unity*) there are a number of smaller trade union organisations like the students' syndicate, the teachers' syndicate, the aviators' syndicate and the state employees' syndicate.

The Independent Syndicates in Bulgaria have broad political orientation. In the transitional period towards democracy this central confederation has maintained political neutrality.

Still in the process of its creation, *Podkrepa* follows the model of Solidarity in Poland. The unions have been built up on both teritorial and branch principles. Such organisations may be active in joint ventures, even those controlled by foreign capital. Trade unions carry out their activities in accordance with Bulgarian law. They are autonomous and independent of the state, employers' unions, the enterprises where their members work, and of any political parties and social movements.

The trade unions aim to co-ordinate the interests of employees and employers, so that the successful functioning of the labour process can be assured. However, the trade unions' fundamental purposes are to defend the rights and interests of their members in relation to labour, employment, living standards, social security and fringe benefits.

In case of labour disputes, the unions may defend their members in the local courts. In the course of the democratisation process in Bulgaria, trade unions have gained more importance. In 1991 a General Agreement was signed between the government, the syndicates and the employers' unions. However, this accord does not operate at present because both *Podkrepa* and the Confederation of Independent Trade Unions withdrew their commitment.

The role of the syndicates in solving questions of vital importance for Bulgarian citizens was originally underestimated by the government of Prime Minister Filip Dimitrov and, as a result, social tension was increased during its first 100 days in office. The government is now reviewing its attitude towards trade unions and intends to negotiate with them in order to achieve social peace.

EMPLOYMENT LAW

Employment relations in Bulgaria are governed by the Labour Code of 1986 (the 'Code') which came into force on 1 January 1987 and a number of related laws. These guarantee an employee minimum standards in relation to health and safety, human rights, holidays and pay. There are also regulations specifically protecting women and young people. The National Assembly is currently reviewing a number of proposed amendments to the Code.

General principles

The maximum working week is 8 hours per day for 5 days per week. The statutory minimum paid holiday is 14 days per annum, although more experienced employees may be entitled to up to 28 days. Employees are paid monthly with the minimum wage (in 1992) set at Lev850 per month (although this changes regularly with inflation). The minimum employment age is 16 years and there are special provisions in the Code entitling young people of between 16 and 18 years to more favourable working conditions. Health and safety requirements are stricter for young people – the maximum working day is 7 hours and the minimum period of paid holiday is 26 working days per annum.

All workers in Bulgaria have the right to be a member of a trade union and to strike. This represents a significant move away from the old command-style regime with accompanying compulsory employment.

Both Bulgarian and foreign nationals can be employed under a foreign law employment contract, but matters not covered in the employment contract of a Bulgarian will be governed by Bulgarian law. If the employer is a foreign person, the provisions of the Bulgarian labour and insurance legislation apply to all employment and social security issues which have not been specifically provided for in the employment contract.

Contracts of employment

Bulgarian contracts of employment may be either collective or individual. The regulations in the Code concerning collective employment contracts are out of date and do not correspond with recent democratic changes.

The Law on the Economic Activity of Foreign Persons and on the Protection of Foreign Investments (the 'FIL') of 16 January 1992 (see Chapter 7) provides that employment relations between a foreign employer and his Bulgarian or foreign employees working in Bulgaria must be governed by a written employment contract. A 'foreign employer' in this context is defined as a company with a foreign participation exceeding 50 per cent, a foreign person registered in Bulgaria as a sole trader or a branch or representative office of a foreign person. Such an employment contract must comply with Bulgarian labour law with regard to:

1. the maximum duration of the working day and the minimum duration of rest periods and paid annual holiday;

2. the minimum wage;

3. the minimum amount of notice for termination and compensation for termination;

4. the employer's liability for damages caused by an accident at work or illness contracted at work; and

5. health and safety regulations.

Under the FIL, Bulgarians working for a foreign employer must be insured at the employer's expense for all insurance risks under Bulgarian social security legislation. Foreigners employed by such a foreign employer must be insured against temporary and permanent disablement at the employer's expense and at a premium of not less than 20 per cent of gross monthly wages. Such foreigners working for a foreign employer are given the right, under the FIL, to convert into foreign currency up to 70 per cent of their wages and benefits received under their employment contracts. This right gives them the attractive opportunity of repatriating their earnings in foreign currency.

Termination of employment

An employee may terminate a contract of employment for an indefinite term by giving one month's notice and without giving reasons. Foreign employers must, under the FIL, give notice of termination of such an employment but they are not obliged to give reasons on termination of employment. On the contrary, a Bulgarian employer has no such right to terminate an employment contract for an indefinite term without giving reasons. Accordingly, most such employers offer fixed-term employment contracts to their employees. These will usually be for one year and can be renewed on a rolling basis. An employer should ensure, however, that the renewal of the contract of employment takes place before it expires because if the employee comes to work the day after expiry (with no new contract) he is automatically deemed to have a contract of employment for an indefinite term.

An employee unfairly dismissed can claim reinstatement before the court, which is entitled to order the employer to re-employ the employee and award salary payments for the period of the contract remaining. There is no award for damages in lieu of reinstatement.

The FIL provides that disputes between foreign employers and Bulgarian citizens are to be settled by the Bulgarian courts. Disputes with foreign employees may be settled in accordance with the terms of the employment contract.

Unfair competition

The Fair Competition Law of 17 May 1991 prohibits breaches of business confidence and the disclosure of commercial secrets. Specifically, employees are prohibited (a) from disclosing an employer's business secrets for at least five years after termination of employment and (b) from working for a competitor or setting up a competitive business either during or within three years after the termination of such employment. In practice, this may be difficult to enforce.

Part III

The Options for British Business

19

Planning

Touche Ross

TAKING A VIEW OF THE MARKET

Bulgaria is situated at an important crossroads in Eastern Europe, at
the centre of the Balkans and between European and Middle Eastern
economies. This allows a broad range of business activities to be
carried out with several neighbouring countries, such as the new
sovereign states of the former Yugoslavia, Romania, Greece, Albania,
Turkey, the Middle East and the Ukraine, Russia, Georgia and
Armenia. It has a highly educated labour force and a considerable
labour price advantage.

Bulgaria has great potential for foreign investment and industrial
co-operation projects. Of particular interest are the agriculture, food
and light industry sectors. There is surplus production capacity in
many branches of the economy including the engineering, electronics, chemical and light industries. Some of these industries are
relatively advanced technologically and have a qualified labour force
with relatively strong research and development capabilities.

Degree of risk

Currently, foreign investment activities are subject to a relatively
high degree of business risk. This risk is principally associated with
the uncertainties surrounding the speed of economic reform attained
by the new democratic government and continuing uncertainty about
economic prospects. Some state-owned companies and other
economic units are financially unstable. There are also problems
with the payment of the country's foreign debt. In addition,
uncertainty surrounds the political environment and, to some
degree, the legal framework. These risks, however, are broadly

comparable with most of the other countries of Eastern Europe, and they are less than in some.

What sort of business environment is it?

The business environment is improving progressively. There are many ambitious and flexible private companies that meet modern international business standards. Many of the state-owned companies are also adapting to business methods more in line with those of foreign investors. Many managers have received training in Western business practices and have an acceptable level of English.

Bulgarian partners

The structure of Bulgarian industry is varied and hence the choice of investment partners is considerable. On the one hand, there are huge state-owned companies (most of them at present joint stock companies solely owned by the state), which have a considerable hold on many important branches of the national economy while, on the other hand, a lot of small private companies conduct successful foreign economic activities, but generally without large production capacity. These latter entities are proving dynamic agents of change and are the seed of new large companies and industries.

The financial health of particular Bulgarian companies should of course be carefully examined, the most reliable source of information being the national commercial banks.

Investment required

The resources needed to establish new activities in Bulgaria will vary between investment projects. The financial support of the foreign partner will probably be fundamental since he will be in a position to provide capital, managerial skills and access to new markets. While in many branches of industry foreign investors will see the need for investment in modern technology, Bulgaria has the advantage that a qualified work-force is available, especially in engineering and technical disciplines.

Key areas of concern

Preliminary studies will be required to assess the viability of any investment or venture in Bulgaria. The foreign investor should obtain sufficient information on the Bulgarian economic situation before initiating contact with potential partners. Foreign investors should also conduct adequate field research when seeking a reliable local partner. Ambitious new private companies offer some attractions, particularly for small projects. Experts working in such companies can be indispensable advisers on a wide range of problems within the country.

For larger investment projects it is advisable to seek a partnership with an experienced Bulgarian company with production, marketing and trade potential, and which can take an active part in the project.

WAYS INTO THE MARKET

Exports

Bulgaria operates a relatively liberal export regime. There are virtually no prohibitions on exports, the few exceptions being commodities for which demand is unsatisfied on the local market. Minimum export prices are established for only a limited number of commodity sub-groups.

The national export promotion system is still at an embryonic stage. However, exports have been considerably stimulated by the high exchange rate of hard currencies against the Bulgarian lev.

Imports

The Bulgarian import regime has been fully liberalised. Import licences are only required for certain commodities, mainly connected with national security and defence and with the international obligations of Bulgaria to control trade of certain prohibited goods.

Bulgaria applies a customs tariff based on the Harmonised System of Coding and Description of Commodities. Tariff duties are imposed at an internationally acceptable level. All imports are subject to a customs' clearance tax equal to 0.5 per cent of the dutiable value.

Licensing and franchising

Licensing and franchising (see Chapter 24) are not yet widely used as forms of business co-operation in Bulgaria. However, licensing is relatively widespread in the areas of technology transfer and trademarks. The number of franchise agreements in trade and tourism is also growing.

Distributorships and leasing

In 1991 the number of foreign companies using local distributors in

Bulgaria increased sharply. The legal framework governing distributorships is favourable. It is, however, important that the rights and obligations of the local partner be clearly defined in the distributorship agreement. The territory within which the distributorship is to be limited must be strictly specified.

Leasing operations are relatively widespread in Bulgaria, particularly in respect of machinery, equipment and motor vehicles. Bulgarleasing, for example, is a leading Bulgarian company which specialises in the leasing industry and may be of interest to foreign companies. Foreign companies should seek and obtain reliable guarantees for payment of leasing instalments by the Bulgarian lessee.

Sub-assembly

Bulgarian companies can be suitable partners for sub-assembly contracts in many branches of activity, including machinery and equipment, electronics and electrotechnics. This is because of their existing spare capacity and of the relatively high qualifications of the labour force.

Tendering for contracts

Tenders from the government are quite rare due to the Bulgarian economic crisis. However, Bulgaria is the beneficiary of a number of investment projects financed by the World Bank, the European Bank for Reconstruction and Development (EBRD) and European Community programmes, where contract tenders are invited. The various publications issued by these institutions may serve as a source of information in respect of such tenders. Contract tendering will become more common once the privatisation process begins in earnest.

TIMING

Bulgaria is a business partner of growing importance and many companies from Western Europe, Greece, Turkey and the Middle East are already present. Competition is therefore expected to increase and for this reason it may be preferable to enter the Bulgarian market as soon as possible with specific projects, well-assessed resources and a proper consideration of business risks. Entering the market in say five years' time may be more difficult, or too late.

Extended time-scales

Depending on the strategy of the foreign investor, extended time-scales for business activities should be developed. Many investors consider Bulgaria to represent a good long-term rather than a short-term investment prospect. In general, it may be advisable for the foreign investor to start with trade operations, developing perhaps into sub-assembly operations and then to direct investment in the Bulgarian economy.

DOING THE DEAL

Every prospective deal or venture should be subject to detailed valuation, including an assessment of all possible risk factors. An important local business characteristic is the change in state regulation of economic activities coupled with the economic reform programme. For this reason feasibility studies should be sensitive to these possible developments.

It is generally easy to negotiate with a Bulgarian company as Western partners will find a good knowledge of the product, an ambitious business plan and a flexible open approach to business. It is however more difficult to negotiate with the bureaucracy – in many cases bureaucrats wish to co-operate, but are not in a position to fully deliver what they promise.

It is compulsory for all transactions with Bulgarian partners to be finalised in writing as specified trade contracts, and, in general, Bulgarian partners have a good record for fulfilling their international contractual obligations. It is, of course, essential that clauses are included in trade contracts against non-fulfilment of obligations. International trade contracts need not be registered with any Bulgarian public institution. However, an important factor in their enforcement will be an appropriately worded arbitration clause.

PUTTING TOGETHER A FINANCIAL PACKAGE

Internationally recognised procedures for assessing the efficiency of financial co-operation and investment projects have been established in Bulgaria. Bulgarian partners can show great creativity in discussing the particular pattern of financial co-operation.

The country's national infrastructure for the use of foreign aid and multilateral loans is still being developed. Most external financial assistance is realised through inter-governmental channels on either a bilateral or multilateral basis.

Bulgaria is the recipient of many international economic aid programmes. The most important are the joint programmes with the IMF, the World Bank and the EBRD. Bulgaria also participates in the EC's special programmes, such as PHARE, INTERREG and TEMPUS. Companies operating in Bulgaria can apply for financial assistance to the State Fund for Reconstruction and Development and to the State Fund For Small and Medium-size Enterprises. Reliable information about foreign economic aid and loans for Bulgaria can be obtained by foreign companies from the countries offering such financial assistance to Bulgaria.

THE PRACTICALITIES OF SETTING UP AN OFFICE

In many cases it may be preferable, when setting up an office in Bulgaria, to work with a local partner. Of particular importance is the choice of a suitable office and a location close to the business centre since this will be close to banks, chambers of trade and other public and business institutions.

To succeed in Bulgarian business, negotiations must be undertaken personally and business contacts maintained. From this point of view your office must be suitable for business visits. Renting office space is relatively inexpensive – from $10 to $20 per square metre per month. It is also important to have an office with reliable communications, including telephone, fax and telex.

STAFF

Some Western firms consider it important to employ expatriates in their offices and branches in Bulgaria, predominantly in management or administrative positions. Expatriates might also be employed to undertake specific engineering, designing, assembling or other similiar operations in production. However, it should be taken into consideration that living conditions are still relatively difficult for foreigners in Bulgaria and that they often experience substantial difficulties with the language.

Local staff are generally well educated, competent and have a good knowledge of the local market and business conditions. When they are well-motivated, Bulgarian employees demonstrate high levels of discipline, creativity, stability, flexibility and adaptability in their work.

For a good technical operator, the average monthly wage is about Lev2500–3000. For a good manager it is approximatively Lev4000–5000. Note, however, that employers must pay an additional 35 per cent of each employee's wage to the social security funds.

20

Marketing
PR Trading

Marketing in Bulgaria is a paradox. The average monthly salary is less than £50, of which 47 per cent is spent on food, and 30 per cent of the population is on a pension of about £20 a month. Meat costs £1–2 a kilo and TV sets sell from £100. Yet it is possible to advertise a slimming cream on TV at £9 a treatment and for pharmacies to sell out next day.

Conservative business executives might reasonably expect that in a deficit economy, the entire concept of marketing could be reduced to the one variable of price. While this is largely true in Bulgaria, it is nonetheless a fast changing market with lucrative gaps. Those companies that are benefiting combine marketing flair with an operational flexibility which accommodates local entrepreneurs alongside western business ethics and discipline.

CONSUMER PRODUCTS

It is in the consumer products sector where the risk–reward ratio is greatest. The transition from an economy in which consumer product availability, choice and price were determined by state bureaucrats to one with consumer-led purchasing power and ultimately consumer discrimination, is the great market challenge in Bulgaria today, as in other former communist countries. It brings to the fore and illustrates the problems of those changing economies most starkly: the creation of consumer awareness, the nurturing of consumer desire, the expectation and the frustration (especially with prices just or totally out of reach), and the consequent creation of a middle class and the despair of the rest.

This is where the changes in the politico-economic system are most closely felt by the population, and where dissatisfaction with the new system begins and ends. How the goods get into the shops and on to the streets, who controls distribution and the price, and how the economy works in practice has to be ascertained by street-wise market research for particular products at a particular time. It is then necessary to be quick and keep control of the situation from a position of knowledge. Success in the market depends also on observing some basic rules of practice:

- Do not enter the market without sufficient back ups of stamina and cash.

- Do not rely on trust. Employ a lawyer in the country but work quickly.

- Gone are the days when a visit to the market every few months was enough. Be absent at your peril.

- Bulgaria is not a pretty little country coming slowly and elegantly to a market economy. It is obeying the rule of the jungle. This is goldrush time.

- The consumer market is controlled by sharp practitioners.

Market research

For the best consumer market research, step out into the streets of Bulgarian cities including, but not only, Sofia. Go with a Bulgarian. Use your eyes and ears and ask questions. Better still go with an expatriate or Western businessman who has known the market over the past, say, four years, plus a Bulgarian, and go often.

Look at the new shops and the new coffee bars, not to mention the street traders selling everything from plumbing parts to whisky, cosmetics to contraceptives – most of it is cheap, of poor quality or recycled but, most importantly, it is there. Find out how it got there. The state shops remain relatively unstocked and unfrequented, so ignore the old monopolistic buying system. Find out who and where and when and how, and don't forget to ask the price. That is, what does it cost to enter?

Obviously look at what is on sale. If the current competition is half your price, and selling well, then do not expect to win a quality argument without heavy promotional costs, and strong branding. Alternatively could you source locally and brand/promote?

Promotion and product mix

Advertising in Bulgaria is well developed – on the TV, in the news-papers, on the trams and buses, on the hoardings and at the point of sale. So if your product is anything other than a commodity it will almost certainly pay to advertise. Create brand loyalty now before your competitors do. The success of Marlboro cigarettes and Johnnie Walker whisky is not due to chance. It is the result of planned (and unplanned) promotional effort and control of distribution to eliminate fakes. In consumer household goods, there is heavy point of sale advertising by Philips and Tefal – the market leaders. For the very limited DIY market, there is Black and Decker. The investment cost at this time is high, but a few companies are making the effort and are likely to still be there when the market has stabilised.

More or less anything can be sold, and the standard of product differentiation – quality, packaging, branding – is generally low. Where there is a locally made product which is still available, it tends to be cheap but perceived to be of low quality whether it is or not. The fact that many factories produce for export means that quality product could be available, especially in the clothing, hosiery and footwear sectors, and for investors who seek a participation in some of those factories there could be real opportunities. Local assembly/part manufacture, especially of consumer household goods and electronics is another area with particular scope for highly priced manufacturing units.

Most imported products, other than a relatively few branded goods, come from Turkey and Greece, and availability overrides poor quality in all cases. Point of sale presentation remains generally poor, except in a few shops where Western style shopfitting has been introduced. This is particularly true in the spawning pharmaceutical sector with well-stocked new pharmacies on a Western level taking over from the state provider.

Distribution

Bulgaria is fast becoming a nation of shopkeepers, traders and wholesalers, and the method of distribution is the same for locally made and imported products. Either the producer controls his own distribution in the country, or he sells to a trader who imports or buys from the plant directly, sells to wholesalers, and retails as well. The vast majority of these operations are now private. There are a few state-owned distribution and importing companies like Transimpex and Raznoiznos which import consumer goods. They, like the private trader/wholesaler, import and sell wholesale but they also have their own shops all over the country from which they retail. Recently, many foreign operators have also entered into the market – mainly Greek, Turkish and Arabian – who sell in their own, or joint venture, shops and also wholesale.

The expanding pharmaceutical sector operates in a similar way – part state, part private. It is constrained by government regulations, which can be expected to increase in order to better control this business to the benefit of the health care system as a whole.

Pricing

Price obviously plays a very large part in the consumption of most products and it is treated as a very blunt tool at the present time.

Customs tariffs are variable by country of origin and by product, and can be high for imported luxury goods. Customs tariffs also depend on whether or not similar goods are locally produced. The whole consumer products sector is liable to turnover tax, although how much of this is actually paid at the present time is questionable.

Some products, including ethical and over-the-counter pharmaceuticals, health foods, cosmetics, and veterinary products require product registration, which can be costly and time consuming.

As regards price as a marketing variable, consignment stocking and one or two-month credit terms are the keys to success. So the supplier who exports a container of goods himself, financing it and effectively wholesaling from bonded or other stores in Bulgaria, will be much more successful than the supplier who expects cash advances or confirmed letters of credit. This implies a considerable investment and, in particular, control of cash and cash transactions and transfers.

Product discounting is almost unheard of, and where it exists it is generally misunderstood and abused. Thus, again in the pharmaceutical sector, one large state wholesaler has been receiving quantity discounts in bonus free goods, which are supposed to be passed on as free goods, but instead have been used to reduce the price by the equivalent margin, thus ruining the market for the producer himself. If you give sophisticated loyalty bonuses and discounts you need to make sure they are properly understood and handled.

Legal, political and economic aspects

The encouragement of privatisation has made the consumer products sector a very active one, and Western companies are at liberty to trade as wholesalers and retailers as long as they register as a Bulgarian company, subject to Bulgarian taxation and laws. The lev, in which trade takes place, is reasonably stable and is internally convertible. Shop property rents are high, due primarily to the Bulgarian phenomenon of restitution – the giving back of property to former owners – and the operation of market forces currently producing unrealistically high prices, especially in Sofia. Be sure to have a rent review clause which allows a rent decrease as well as an increase.

Construction and the shopfitting industry are also important private sector activities, and shop reconstruction and fitting to a reasonable level of both style and quality is now possible.

INDUSTRIAL GOODS – CAPITAL AND CONSUMABLE

On the face of it, little has changed in the marketing of capital and consumable goods to industry except that the Foreign Trade Organisation ('FTO') structure has largely broken down and sales are to be made generally direct with the factories/organisations. The problem is that these organisations themselves are in a state of chaos, often awaiting privatisation but, in the meantime, without experienced leaders. Add to that the fact that there is little money available except in specific sectors and that there are few if any Western credits and the picture is a gloomy one. This is especially so for companies relying on capital goods sales to Bulgaria – many factories are closed because of lack of working capital or no market for their goods, or both.

Marketing mix

All aspects of the marketing mix of the capital goods industry are relevant once your market research shows that there is a market for the product. In the consumer product sector, a local agent is particularly useful – to keep your products in the market-place and to be looking for the time when there is money in a particular sector. Bear in mind that the agent will not be making any money at this introductory stage, and therefore you will have to work on a retainer agreement in order to encourage him to do any work at all. This will still be cheaper than going solo into the market (although it would probably pay to attend the autumn or spring fair in Plovdiv, both to keep abreast of the market and to support the agent).

Marketing for aid programmes

There is little or no money in the state/capital goods sector, but there is money from the UK, the EC and US sources for technical assistance in all its many forms, including consultancy, training and equipment/systems purchase.

A different type of marketing approach is needed to secure business in this sector, and the company seriously intent on tapping such funding sources is well advised to set up a marketing team to research fully what is on offer, and how it is awarded. In other words, apply a full marketing strategy to the business of getting the money as well as the business of selling the product.

It is important to get to know the relevant organisations providing aid, and the objectives of the aid programmes. Find out what is going to be on offer and how it is going to be awarded. Ensure that your organisation qualifies to participate and that the aid agencies and the recipients know you, and that the package you can offer is tailored to the need as perceived by them.

Product, place and price mix

Make sure you know what is going to be bought, and get involved at the specification stage if it is an equipment purchase. Be there often, and make sure both the awarding and recipient countries fully understand what you can offer. Finally, find out the criteria on which the tenders will be judged, and be flexible.

The lack of funding and Western credits has hit the industrial goods sector badly, as has the need to redirect industrial effort. Privatisation is talked about rather than enacted, and has not yet injected any growth into the sector. Aid programmes offer the best short and medium-term opportunities and should themselves be approached with full regard to the best professional marketing strategy for success.

21

Agencies and Distributorships

Sinclair Roche & Temperley

Frequently, potential foreign investors in a new market seek to 'test the water' through the creation of an agency or distribution arrangement, rather than proceeding with a direct investment by way of a joint venture or, possibly, the formation of a local subsidiary company. Normally, the risks involved in an agency or distribution arrangement are perceived to be significantly less than, for example, the incorporation of a local company. Also, if unsuccessful, it is usually easier to terminate an agency or distribution arrangement than to go through the full process of winding up a local subsidiary company.

The purpose of this chapter is to consider agency and distribution arrangements as an alternative to the full process of incorporation and to provide a brief outline of the relevant Bulgarian legislation affecting such business structures.

AGENCY

The concept of agency exists in Bulgaria and is embodied in and governed by the Commercial Law of 16 May 1991 (the 'Commercial Law').

The Commercial Law recognises the basic structure of the agent being authorised by written agreement (which should be registered in the Commercial Register), to act on behalf of a principal in connection with the principal's business activities within a specified area. The applicable law of the agency agreement is the law of the country where the agent carries on business, regardless of the place where the agreement is concluded; accordingly, if a Bulgarian agent is appointed to do business in Bulgaria, then Bulgarian law must apply and the agency agreement cannot provide otherwise. The agency agreement may provide a forum (for example an arbitration procedure) or jurisdiction in respect of disputes arising from the agency.

The Commercial Law outlines the obligations of both principal and agent and makes provision for the payment of commission even in the absence of such a provision in the agency agreement. The law also provides for an agent to receive commission after termination of the agreement in a situation where the principal continues to extract profit from a client provided by the agent. It has been suggested, however, that it may be possible to exclude the right to receive commission by special contractual terms.

Provision is made for the principal to impose reasonable restrictive covenants upon the agent after termination of the agency agreement. However, the law does allow the agent to act for more than one principal as long as they are not in direct competition with one another.

An agent is free to enter into an agreement or series of agreements on behalf of the principal even without his knowledge and, once notified to the principal, a contract thus entered into will be considered to have been confirmed unless the principal renounces the contract immediately upon receipt of notification from either the agent or the third party and advises them of the renunciation.

It is significant that the Commercial Law provides that the scope of the authority and all arrangements between a principal and an agent must be the subject of a written agreement. This agreement must be notified to and registered with the local Commercial Register.

Termination of an agency agreement is usually by consensus. However, there must be an application to the court to strike the registration of the agreement from the Commercial Register.

ATTORNEYS

The Commercial Law recognises an attorney as a person authorised by a sole trader to engage in activities enumerated in the power of attorney (this can be extended to the conduct of all the trader's usual business) for fixed remuneration. The main distinction between an agent and an attorney is the more limited nature of the attorney's powers and the absence of a commission. The power of attorney is usually limited in that it applies to a single individual and may not be transferred to or confer powers upon a third party. Any contravention by the attorney of the limits of his authority can expose him to an action for damages by the principal, or alternatively, a declaration that any unauthorised contract with a third party is entered into on the attorney's own account. A sole trader must lodge such a claim against an attorney within a month of discovering or being informed of such an unauthorised contract and must have notified the third party, not later than one year after the conclusion of the contract.

As with an agency contract, a power of attorney must be notified and registered at the Commercial Register and, if the power of attorney is withdrawn, the necessary procedure should be followed to remove it from the register.

Both agents and attorneys are under the same duty to maintain the confidentiality and good name of their principals.

REPRESENTATIVE OFFICES

Under Bulgarian law, one of the most popular types of enterprise is a representative office. For example, a potential investor may often set up a representative office in Bulgaria and appoint a third party to act as his local agent or branch manager (see Chapter 25).

Under the 1992 Foreign Investment Law, foreign persons who are entitled to engage in business activities under their national legislation may establish commercial representations in Bulgaria. The only official requirement which accompanies such an establishment is a necessity to register the representative office with the local Commercial Register and the Minister of Finance. The representative office itself is, however, not a legal entity and may not conduct business in Bulgaria. Such activities are carried out by the local agent or branch manager.

DISTRIBUTORSHIP

The distinction between a distributor and an agent is recognised under Bulgarian law which classifies a distributor as a 'dealer'.

The Commercial Law does not apply to dealers. The applicable law is the LOC, although it is expected that there will be a future supplement to the Commercial Law to cover this area. Reference is made to the section on the sale and purchase of goods under the LOC summaries in Chapter 8.

The overriding problem with the use of distributorships in Bulgaria is the transfer of ownership of goods. Under the LOC, a dealer cannot sell goods unless he has unencumbered title to them. Accordingly, if there is any retention of title clause in the distributorship agreement as security for the principal (a normal provision in Western agreements), the distributorship would be unworkable under Bulgarian law.

22

Export and Import

Touche Ross

TRADE LIBERALISATION WITHIN THE REFORM PROGRAMME

In the past, Bulgaria relied on state trading and managed foreign trade through import and export quotas and a small number of registered foreign trade companies. Domestic producers were insulated from changes in export and import prices through a complicated system of multiple exchange rates which ensured that prices of imports and exports for the domestic producer equalled domestic prices.

The oligopolistic structure of domestic markets at the outset of economic reform has made it unlikely that meaningful market prices can emerge in a number of sectors in the absence of foreign competition. An open trade regime combined with a reasonably stable exchange rate are expected to allow the 'importation' of world market prices to which the Bulgarian economy needs to adapt.

Foreign trade regulations have become one of the main, and probably the most successful, areas of structural reform in Bulgaria since February 1991. The complete liberalisation of the trade regime was considered to be the prerequisite for the full integration of the country into the international economic system. To support this process, additional measures were introduced. Foreign trade rights were granted to all enterprises, and not only to foreign trade organisations which carried out state trade before importers were given free access to foreign exchange on presentation of order papers through the inter-bank market. According to the provisions of currency exchange regulations, merchant banks are now allowed to freely sell unlimited amounts of hard currency to Bulgarian companies, against documents certifying the necessity of payments for imports of goods and services, transport and other related expenditures, business tours, insurance fees and other fees related to imported goods.

Since the beginning of 1991, import and export regulations have progressed towards liberalisation. Bulgaria's trade regime is now such that price-based measures (tariffs, exchange rates) are the major policy instruments.

An important element of the liberalisation measures was the abolition of the licensing regime, which is now applied only in a few specific cases. The restrictions apply to a specific commodity or service and not to a specific producer or consumer.

Council of Ministers Decree 114 of 25 June 1992 is the principal statutory instrument regulating the foreign trade regime. The export, import and re-export of military equipment is the subject of special treatment.

IMPORT REGULATION

Tariffs

All goods carried across the Bulgarian border are subject to customs control.

The import customs tariff system is based on the Harmonised Customs Tariff adopted by the Customs Co-operation Council, which is applied in most countries.

Bulgaria applies a Generalised System of Preferences, which sets lower tariffs on imports from the developing countries. Imports originating from the 42 least developed countries qualify for duty-free treatment in Bulgaria. For all other imports, duty is charged according to a two-column tariff schedule which entered into force on 1 June 1992. The amount of duty depends on the origin of the goods.

Column one applies to imports originating from countries which qualify for preferential duty treatment in Bulgaria. These preferential rates apply to 118 developing countries. Column two concerns imports from 44 countries which have a most favoured nation (MFN) trading status with Bulgaria. About 80 per cent of total Bulgarian imports are charged under column two.

Imports originating from countries having neither preferential nor most favoured nation status are charged with duty of an amount equal to twice the corresponding amount under column two.

The new tariff schedule, introduced in June 1992, has only 5 tariff rates, which range from 5 per cent to 40 per cent.

For the last 10 years customs duties have stayed at their 1981 level as agreed at the Tokyo Round of multilateral trade negotiations within the framework of the General Agreement on Trade and Tariffs (GATT). By implementing the new schedule the average trade-weighted tariff increased from about 8 per cent to 17 per cent. Under the old code the tariff on imports of industrial products was 6.9 per cent while, under the new code, the average tariff is 16.7 per cent. The equivalent figures for agricultural products are 17.4 per cent under the old code and 25.8 per cent under the new tariff code. The cited rates apply to MFN countries.

Bulgaria gained the status of an observer country in GATT in 1967 and, since 1986, a procedure for joining GATT has been underway. Since the country is not yet a member of GATT, it has more flexibility to restructure its tariff schedule.

The almost complete liberalisation of the trade regime poses the question of trade protection for Bulgarian enterprises since unfettered import competition may risk wiping out firms and industries before they have had a chance to adapt to the new environment. As a result of the new tariff schedule, the desired level of import protection has been achieved through a slight increase in import tariffs, a measure with an additional advantage of generating Budget revenues.

The following items are exempt from customs duties until the end of 1992: medical child foodstuffs, agricultural machinery and spare parts, pesticides and fertilisers, ready-made medical and diagnostic forms having no domestic analogues, raw materials and substances for the manufacturing of medical and diagnostic forms. For some goods, including sugar, rice and ready-made medical and diagnostic forms, minimal duties of 3 per cent and 5 per cent are imposed, depending on the tariff schedule column.

Import duties are payable within 30 days from the date of entry of the goods into Bulgaria.

Import customs valuation is based on the negotiated purchase price as denominated in foreign currency, cif the Bulgarian border. The dutiable value of imported goods comprises the purchase price, transport expenditure, insurance fees and all other expenditures connected with transportation such as loading, unloading etc. For this purpose the following documents have to be submitted:

■   invoice and goods specification;

- freight documents;

- insurance policy; and

- certificate of origin.

The foreign currency value of the imported goods is translated into leva according to the central exchange rate of the Bulgarian National Bank at the date of entry of the goods into Bulgarian territory. An additional levy of 0.5 per cent of the dutiable value on the imported goods is collected in order to finance the customs process.

The import of eight commodity groups, including pesticides, fertilisers, ferrous and non-ferrous metals, leather shoes, clothing, textiles, cellulose and paper, coal, electric power, oil, fuel oil, gas oil and spirits is subjected to a registration regime. Registration should be completed within one day of the importer's application and simply represents an information gathering device for the purposes of the Ministry of Trade.

Import licensing requirements

Import licences are required only for imports of goods subject to inter-governmental agreements, trade protocols, clearing agreements and the import of goods against payment in leva. Additional to this group are the following:

- ready-made medical and diagnostic forms, substances and raw materials for their production, stomalogical materials;

- narcotic substances and resources for their production;

- cigarettes and cigars;

- radioactive materials, applied in medicine and industry;

- dangerous substances, wastes and technologies which are damaging to the environment;

- gunpowder, explosives and related materials destined for civil purposes;

- hunting and sporting weapons and ammunition;

- rare and precious metals and stones, rough and solutions; and

- wild animals and plants specified in the Washington Convention.

Import quotas and taxes

The import regime in Bulgaria is almost completely liberalised in this area. Import quotas were introduced only for tobacco, oranges, tangerines, bananas and ice-cream. The temporary 15 per cent import surcharge on overall imports was removed in May 1992. Import tax is imposed on 12 goods, mainly foodstuffs and cosmetics. They vary from 5 per cent to 25 per cent.

Turnover tax

Imports for final consumption attract turnover tax or excise duty. Both companies and sole traders who import goods and services aimed at further sale are subjected to tax. The tax rate is based on the total of the customs dutiable value, the customs duty and the customs clearance charge. In other words, the taxation basis of imported goods includes all kinds of taxes, duties, commissions, insurance and freight which have been paid abroad. The liability arises on the day a commercial invoice is rendered or, if there is no invoice, from the day on which payment is effected.

Most imported goods aimed at further sale are subject to turnover tax at 22 per cent. Some goods of extreme importance such as milk, common bread, electricity, hard coal and devices for the disabled are exempted from tax. Some foodstuffs, such as dairy products, flour, meat, poultry, fish, vegetables and fruit are charged to turnover tax at 10 per cent.

Excise duty

The sale of some luxury goods or those considered detrimental to health (both domestic and imported goods) are subjected to excise duty. Those goods which are charged with excise duty are not also subject to turnover tax.

The highest excise tax of 70 per cent is applied with reference to whisky, heavy drinks, jewellery and precious metals. The 60 per cent rate applies to perfume in aerosol, tobacco and cigarettes. Leather-wear, furcoats and brandy are charged at 50 per cent. Wine, beer, coffee, tea, video equipment, matches and gas lighters are taxed at 40 per cent.

Excise duties on liquid fuels have recently been reduced and vary at present between 10 per cent (propane) and 40 per cent (gasoline).

Documentation

In its trade practice, Bulgaria utilises the various uniform internationally accepted documents, such as:

- commercial invoices;
- certificates of origin;
- insurance policies;
- bills of lading;
- international consignment notes; and
- bills of exchange.

EXPORT REGULATION

Export licensing requirements and quotas

No special licence is required except for the following exports:

- goods subject to inter-governmental agreements, trade protocols, clearing agreements, and the export of goods against payment in leva;
- tobacco and tobacco products, rare and precious metals and stones (rough and processed) as well as their salts and solutions;
- logs;
- wastes from ferrous and non-ferrous metals;
- objects of archeological, historical, artistic or antiquarian value;
- protected plants and animal species, as well as wild animals and plants listed in the Washington Convention;
- narcotic substances;
- radioactive materials, applied in medicine and industry;
- gunpowder, explosives and related materials designed for civil purposes;
- hunting and sporting weapons and ammunition.

For export licences to be obtained in respect of the above mentioned goods, approval must also be obtained from an appropriate governmental body (ministry or committee).

Licences are also required for the export of goods subject to import quotas under agreements signed by the Republic of Bulgaria. For example, exports of goods within the quotas determined in the agreements between Bulgaria and the EC and Canada are subject to export licensing. Such quotas are applied for exports of textiles to the markets of the EC and Canada, for exports of small cattle and meat thereof for the EC and for exports of ferrous metals and products thereof for the EC. The distribution of quotas among exporters is carried out on a competition basis by the Ministry of Trade. No more than 35 per cent of the quota volume will be allocated to a single exporter. Up to 20 per cent of the quota volume is distributed by the Minister of Trade at his personal discretion.

As a temporary measure until the end of 1992, export quotas apply in respect of wine grapes, bread grain, coarse grain, wheat flour, black oil-bearing sunflower, female animals for breeding purposes, small cattle, raw hides and skins from small cattle, cattle and pigs.

The export of seven commodity groups is subject to registration with the Ministry of Trade. They include live animals, meat and poultry, dairy products, vegetable oils, wine and brandy, rose oil, ferrous and non-ferrous metals, oil, coal, electric power, fuel oils, and gas oil.

Export taxes

From July 1992, Bulgarian exports are no longer subject to any export tax. However, an additional levy of 0.5 per cent of the dutiable value of the exported goods is collected to fund the customs process.

The process of liberalisation of the trade regime in Bulgaria has made great progress, non-tariff instruments being drastically reduced. The full liberalisation of the import and export of services is planned to be carried out in the near future. Obviously future changes will be influenced by the priorities in the structural policy of the government as well as the progress of the country's association agreement with the EC and the procedure for joining GATT.

At present it is not the state of the Bulgarian trade regime that hampers the advancement and reorientation of the country's exports and imports. The most crucial trade policy factor seems to be the improvement of access to Western markets.

23

Trade Finance

East European Projects Consultants

In the 1970s and early 1980s Bulgaria pursued a very cautious policy in regard to the hard currency balance of payments, combined with a willingness to trade with the West that was in contrast to the other Comecon states. The last years of the communist regime, however, saw a reversal of this policy, with a 'dash for growth' which overtaxed the country's earning powers. The result was default by the National Bank (through its Foreign Trade Bank) in servicing its foreign debt.

At over US$12 billion, with a population of under 9 million, the per capita foreign debt is one of the highest in Eastern Europe and severely restricts the government's ability to deal with the current economic problems.

Virtual internal convertibility of the lev was introduced in 1991, and an initial severe devaluation was accepted (from approximately Lev3 for £1 in 1989, to Lev 5.50 at the end of 1990 and nearly Lev40.00 at the end of 1991). In recent months the rate has been fairly steady, but only at the expense of the people's living standards.

FOREIGN EXCHANGE

From the point of view of the trader, foreign exchange is freely available. Amounts up to US$ 0.5 million can normally be purchased within two days, and market rates do not fluctuate wildly. There is still a black market for currency conversion, but its rates are sometimes less favourable than the official market. For practical purposes the lev is convertible, and hard currency payments can be made by Bulgarian companies in the ordinary course of their business without significant delays. Transfers by Bulgarian banks have in the past been notoriously slow, but the introduction of the

Swift system has already brought about a significant improvement locally, and overseas transfers are likely to improve rapidly.

EXPORTING TO BULGARIA

Payment terms

Exporters to Bulgaria are at present likely to insist on no risk payment terms (confirmed irrevocable letter of credit – CILC – or cash before shipment). Because of the National Bank's default, and the parlous state of the economy, Bulgarian banks do not find it possible to arrange for confirmation of their letters of credit (L/Cs) on the strength of their own balance sheets. In some countries (eg Germany) it is possible for the importer to provide hard currency cash cover for a CILC, though it can take 5–6 weeks for an L/C to be opened, even using the Western correspondent of the Bulgarian bank concerned.

In the UK, banks do not normally accept cash cover as sufficient backing for the confirmation of an L/C, so UK exporters normally insist on advance payment. This is largely acceptable for importers who have the funds, though some may require a bank guarantee of performance from the exporter.

Credit lines

For the reasons indicated above, and the losses incurred on East European loans in the recent past, the ordinary small and medium-sized exporter is unlikely to obtain any credit line from UK banks to support sales to Bulgaria as such – as opposed to lines made available to known banking customers in the normal course of business. Factoring and bill discounting (forfait) facilities, being alternatives to credit lines, are also not available. Similarly credit insurance is very unlikely to be obtainable – hence the normal insistence on fully secured transactions.

It is said that German banks, for example, are more willing to provide trade and project finance for business with the East in general (including Bulgaria). Evidence of this is hard to come by, and a previous relationship with the bank is likely to be necessary, except in the case of very large projects.

Credit references

These are becoming more useful in Bulgaria as in the other Eastern

European states, now that there are more non-state companies operating. The introduction in Bulgaria of a new Accounting Law modelled on West European practice will result in more meaningful accounts being available from this year than in the past. As Western credit reference specialists become more active in the region, so Bulgarian companies are becoming more accustomed to being asked for information about their assets and results – and are slowly losing their reluctance to answer such questions. It will, however, take several years at least before anything like a full credit reference service is available.

Western companies active in this field find that they have to build their own information sources, which may include local companies that are beginning to specialise in the provision of information to Western requirements. The Bulgarian banking system is badly in need of modernisation, and banks are generally not a useful source of credit information.

Countertrade

The mainstay of the communist regime's trade with the West, countertrade, is virtually dead. The Bulgarian importer may (rarely) ask for it, but there is no need or justification for such a request. Hard currency is available without much difficulty, at a reasonably stable exchange rate, and the UK exporter would do well to treat any request for countertrade as an offer of sale quite separate from his exports.

IMPORTING FROM BULGARIA

Traders

There are a large number of small trading companies that have sprung up in Bulgaria since the change of regime. Because of the high interest rates, trading is at present much more attractive than production for anyone planning to build a business. There is a clear difference between those companies which have Western business experience, often with managers who have lived in the West, and those with a purely Bulgarian background, who may not even have their own good translator/interpreter. All are, however, likely to offer all types of product for export, even those which have chosen an area in which they wish to specialise.

There remain, of course, many state companies which are

continuing to trade as before, and seeking to expand in the new situation (in preparation for privatisation). In many cases, though by no means all, these companies have lost some of their most experienced managers to the private sector, as well as to the 'political pruning' of top management which unfortunately still takes place and deprives the economy of part of the nation's business talent.

Producers

Producers (industrial and agricultural) who are no longer supported by the old state foreign trade organisations or their own exporting departments – and these are the majority – will often seek to export through agents, often the traders described above, but sometimes through companies with no obvious connection with the goods offered. Agencies are still obtained through contacts, often without reference to the likely success of the agent.

Some producers are still not organised in any way to export, but nevertheless would like to do so. In these cases, the best approach is probably to introduce them to a known local trader, who can at least provide the basic shipping and documentation services.

Prices and performance

The lack of clear organisation of producers and traders dealing in a wide variety of products leads to problems of two kinds with prices. On the one hand it is often difficult to know how many agents there are between the foreign buyer and the producer – and therefore how competitive quoted prices are. Many quotes offered by traders are on plain paper with no reference to a producer; this does not necessarily mean that they cannot be taken seriously, but it is a clear indication of the need for caution.

On the other hand, producers are inclined to increase prices, sometimes very considerably, on receipt of a serious enquiry based on a quote. The only defence against such practices is probably to deal only with traders known and respected by the buyer or a reliable associate.

THE FUTURE

No significant improvement in the trading climate can be expected until international agreement is finally reached on rescheduling

Bulgarian debts. This should provide the conditions for more substantial credits from the West, without which confidence will not increase.

Once this is achieved, the banking system is one of the priority areas for modernisation, together with the communications infrastructure. Clearly this will not happen overnight, but the mechanical side of trading relationships can be expected to improve steadily.

The problem of traders and producers is likely to ease as society settles down to the new conditions, though this could be a slow process. Agriculture is unlikely to prosper as before until the new, private, smaller-scale producers lose their mistrust of anything that smacks of the old regime, including the notion of co-operatives, and join in some effective selling organisation. Industrial activity has to be largely rebuilt, and part of that process is likely to be the incorporation of some of the experienced traders into producer organisations. The timing of this process must be very uncertain.

What is certain is that Bulgaria will remain a country which has the necessary conditions for increasing exports: wages are likely to remain low for the foreseeable future, even in relation to neighbouring countries; there are rich resources for agriculture and tourism; and its geographical and psychological position between East and West has contributed to and will continue to strengthen Bulgaria's trading performance.

24

Licensing and Franchising
Sinclair Roche & Temperley

In entering into a new and developing market, businesses will, in many cases, be reluctant to take the step of establishing a full corporate structure but may be prepared to proceed with a transfer of technology by way of licensing of intellectual property rights or know-how. In this way, the licensor may, through the licensee, be able to manufacture products at a significantly reduced cost to that which would be incurred if the licensed products were to be manufactured outside the developing territory. The licensee will have access to modern technology which should, in turn, assist in the creation of a more market-oriented manufacturing infrastructure.

This chapter is intended to assess the current (and, in some respects, prospective) legal framework in Bulgaria for licensing of intellectual property rights and also considers in outline the legal situation in the country in so far as it may affect the establishment of a business through a franchise relationship.

LICENSING

Often, Western licensors will license intellectual property rights, technology and know-how into Bulgaria under the terms of a licence agreement governed by their own law. Alternatively, Bulgarian law may be used, in which case the general law of contract will apply. This is dealt with in the summary of the Law on Obligations and Contracts in Chapter 8.

Of course, where intellectual property rights are involved, Western licensors will want to ensure that adequate protection is available in Bulgaria so as to reduce the risk of local infringement or plagiarism. The following is a summary of the available protection provided by current Bulgarian law.

Trade and service marks

Trade and service marks are protected through registration at the Institute of Inventions and Innovations in Sofia. Once registered, an exclusive right to use a trade mark is recognised with effect from the day of filing the request for registration at the Institute. This right extends for a period of 10 years and may be extended for additional periods of 10 years provided that the request for extension is made within the final 12 months of validity of the then existing registration or not later than 6 months following expiry of the registration. The extended period will run from the date of expiry of the previous protected term.

Transfer may be effected by assignment or, where a limited interest only is being transferred, through licensing by a licensor.

Foreign persons may apply to the Institute for registration through the Bulgarian Chamber of Commerce and, in the event of a successful application, the protection afforded to a foreign party will be identical to that afforded to a Bulgarian citizen or legal entity. The Institute may refuse to register a trade or service mark or to extend an existing registration. In such circumstances, the party applying for registration may appeal against the refusal before the Sofia City Court, provided that such appeal is lodged within three months of the date of receipt of the notice of refusal.

Patents

Current legislation allows for registration of a patent in respect of any invention and for protection in respect of such registered patent for a period of 15 years from the date of filing of the application. In common with trade and service marks, patent applications are filed with the Institute of Inventions and Innovations in Sofia.

New draft legislation is currently under consideration by the Bulgarian National Assembly that will require patent applications to be filed with a new Patent Office in Sofia. It is intended that the protection afforded by registration will be extended to 20 years from the date of filing of the application and, between application and granting of a patent, interim protection will be afforded on the basis of the specification of the application.

All rights in registered patents are transferable either by licence for the use of a patent or by assignment in respect of all rights in the patent. In order to perfect any licence or assignment, the contract or document evidencing the transfer must be registered at the Institute.

It should also be noted that the new draft legislation provides that, where an invention is of considerable importance to the national economy and where such invention is not being used by the patentee, or where it bears directly on the public interest and no agreement has been reached with the patentee as to use of the patent rights, a compulsory licence may be obtained by any interested governmental body. Thus, parties holding foreign patents and seeking protection in Bulgaria should consider whether or not the particular patent is likely to be affected by such proposed legislation.

Copyright

Works of literature, science and art can be protected by copyright which is regulated by the Press Committee of the Council of Ministers. Protection lasts for the lifetime of the author of the work which is protected by copyright and extends for a further period of 50 years from the first day of January in the year following the death of the author.

Registered designs

External fashioning of any item or article consisting of changes in form, design, decoration or combination of colour (or similar change) can be protected through registration of the design at the Institute of Inventions and Innovations in Sofia.

Upon registration, an exclusive right to use the design is granted from the date of filing for a period of five years. In common with trade marks and patents, rights may be transferred by the granting of a licence or by assignment of all rights in the design.

Know-how

Know-how cannot be registered but may be protected by contract and the application of the general laws of fair competition found in the Fair Competition Law of 17 May 1991 (summarised in Chapter 8). Unfair competition (including using or divulging a third party's trade secrets contrary to good faith and normal practice) is illegal and claims in respect of infringement may be lodged in the local District Court. The court has full powers to suppress the infringement and may order that any profits made in respect of such infringement be appropriated in favour of the state.

FRANCHISING

A franchise is often an extension of the licensing concept, whereby one party makes available to another particular marketing or trading know-how which may (or may not) be protected by intellectual property rights. Many chains of international fast-food restaurants are franchises.

Applicable Bulgarian law in respect of a franchise agreement is found in the Law on Obligations and Contracts and in the Fair Competition Law summarised in Chapter 8. These govern the laws of contract, sale of goods and infringements of marketing or trade secrets. To the extent that the franchise involves the use of intellectual property rights (for example an internationally recognised trade name or marketing formula), protection in Bulgaria can be obtained as outlined earlier in this chapter.

25

Forming a Company
Sinclair Roche & Temperley

The formation of a company for investment in Bulgaria is governed by two pieces of legislation: the Commercial Law of 18 June 1991 (the 'Commercial Law') and the Law on the Economic Activity of Foreign Persons and on the Protection of Foreign Investments of 1 February 1992 (the 'FIL').

Under the FIL there are four types of vehicle available to foreign investors: a branch or representative office; an enterprise formed under the Commercial Law; a joint venture and an agency or distributorship. A minimum investment of Lev50,000 (approximately US$2,300) must be deposited with a Bulgarian bank before a Bulgarian private limited company may be registered. In principle, the company may conduct any type of business. However, where it is controlled by a foreign person, it may need a permit issued by the Council of Ministers for investments in particular areas (see Chapter 7).

Most foreign investors in Bulgaria will make their investment through the vehicle of a branch or representative office or a private limited company and so this chapter will concentrate on the formation of these enterprises.

BRANCH OFFICE

A branch or representative office is a Bulgarian extension of an existing business carried on elsewhere. It is not a separate legal entity and is usually represented by a local manager.

On its establishment, a branch or representative office must be registered at the Commercial Register of the local District Court, giving particulars of its name, registered office, purpose and capital.

Details of the branch manager must also be given and a copy of the certificate of establishment of the foreign principal must also be filed. Within 30 days of the establishment of the business in Bulgaria, the foreign investor must register the branch/representative office with the Minister of Finance on the form prescribed under the FIL.

ESTABLISHMENT OF A BULGARIAN ENTERPRISE

Under the Commercial Law, the following enterprises may be established for the conduct of business in Bulgaria:

1.   an unlimited partnership ('SIE');

2.   a limited partnership ('KD');

3.   a private limited company ('OOD');

4.   a public limited company ('AED'); and

5.   a public limited partnership ('KDA').

Unlimited liability will most likely deter most foreign investors from choosing a Bulgarian partnership as an investment vehicle. The public limited company has the advantage that its shares are freely transferable and may be listed on a stock exchange, but it is not the ideal vehicle for private investment. It is the vehicle that the Bulgarian government will use in the privatisation programme (see Chapter 13). The vehicle most likely to be used by foreign investors who require independence or have outgrown a branch or representative office is the private limited company.

INCORPORATION OF A BULGARIAN PRIVATE LIMITED COMPANY

Capital

Any one or more persons is free to incorporate a private limited company and their liability is limited to the extent of the capital contribution. A private limited company must have a minimum capital of Lev50,000. Contributions of capital may be in cash or in kind. However, if in kind, the contribution must be valued by experts appointed by the District Court.

Articles

The constitution of a Bulgarian private limited company is contained in its articles of association. The Commercial Law provides that these shall state:

1. its business name and registered office;

2. its purpose and duration;

3. the names or the business names of the members;

4. its authorised capital. If there is any unpaid capital at the time of the company's incorporation, the articles must state the terms and conditions for future calls;

5. details of the shares;

6. the manner of its management and representation;

7. any privileges of its members; and

8. any other rights and obligations of the members.

A Bulgarian private limited company is more akin to what many Western businessmen would call an association than a limited company. For example, new members are admitted on application and acceptance by the general meeting; members are entitled to participate in management; membership is terminated on death, dismissal or bankruptcy of the member; transfers of shares among members are free but to new members only after the approval of the general meeting is obtained; and the general meeting may resolve to require additional cash contributions from members to cover losses or temporary cash needs.

Management

A private limited company is managed by its managing director or board of directors in accordance with the Commercial Law and the resolutions of the general meeting. The general meeting's powers include amendment of the articles; the acceptance and dismissal of members; the increase or reduction of capital and the acquisition or disposal of real property, which powers must be exercised by a unanimous vote of members. Other powers of the general meeting, exercised by majority vote, include approval of the accounts; the appointment, removal and remuneration of the directors; commencement of litigation against the directors; and the request of additional capital from members.

Registration

In order to register a private limited company in the Commercial Register, the company must:

1. submit its articles of association;

2. appoint a managing director or board of directors;

3. have at least one-third of each member's share, but not less than Lev500 per member, paid up; and

4. have at least 70 per cent of its authorised share capital paid up.

In practice, the Bulgarian lawyer appointed by the promoters of the company will see to all the formalities and file the articles, particulars of the directors and details of the payment of the minimum capital at the Commercial Register of the local District Court. Thereafter it takes about one month to obtain a registration certificate. Once the registration papers have been lodged, the company can start trading and obtain a certificate to this effect from the District Court. However, its directors are jointly and severally liable for its actions until the incorporation is complete.

As in the case of a branch/representative office, the FIL requires that upon the establishment of a company controlled by a foreign person, the investment must be registered in the prescribed manner with the Minister of Finance within 30 days.

26

Financing and Investment

SG Warburg

Western interest in Bulgaria started before the economic reform programme was implemented in 1991, although few substantial investments were made until recently. In 1989 there were 47 joint ventures established with Bulgarian enterprises and, despite the considerable political and economic uncertainty, by the end of 1990 their number had grown to 110, most of which were with European partners. Although legislation was less favourable for wholly-owned subsidiaries, 60 foreign firms had set up branches in Bulgaria and there were over 200 foreign representative offices by the end of 1990. In 1991, the number of joint venture projects registered in Bulgaria was 450.

VALUATION ISSUES

Under the 1992 Foreign Investment Law ('FIL'), Western firms can own Bulgarian companies and set up their own enterprises. In addition, the FIL removed an important obstacle to foreign investment by allowing the repatriation of profits.

Western firms are still slow in making investment decisions due to the difficulty of valuing Bulgarian enterprises. There are a number of uncertainties inherent in Bulgaria's current economic situation, which make any business plan and thus expected future profits, difficult to predict. The high level of inflation and interest rates make discounted cash flow methods potentially misleading. Furthermore, there is little agreement on which indicator, such as an earnings multiple or a discount to net asset value, should be used in the absence of a reference stock market and considering the limited number of transactions on which information is publicly available.

Lastly, it is difficult to place emphasis on historical data as company accounts seldom give an accurate picture of the value of a business. In addition to the existence of several price distortions, until 1991 Bulgarian accounting legislation differed significantly from international GAAP, making comparisons with Western firms difficult. In particular, assessing the profitability of a Bulgarian business is complex since cash flow statements are not required.

FOREIGN INTEREST

In 1991 and 1992, as a result of the foreign investment laws, an increasing number of multinational companies became active in Bulgaria including Siemens, Schering, Motorola, Texaco, Shell, Westinghouse, Electrolux, IKEA, Scania, Citroën, etc. Many of these companies have entered the Bulgarian industrial sector, attracted by the numerous under-utilised manufacturing facilities. They have been encouraged by the good prospects for economic growth, and on that basis they have shown interest in a long-term commitment. However, as many external observers believe, Bulgaria's strongest selling point has been its very well-educated and low-cost work-force. According to a US consultancy firm, the skill-to-wage ratio of the Bulgarian labour force ranks among the highest in the world.

Foreign interest so far has been most prominent in the automotive sector. Under the Comecon system of country specialisation, the lift-truck industry was assigned to Bulgaria, which developed the largest capacity in the world. This was achieved at the expense of developing the automobile industry and, until recently, Bulgaria relied on assembly of cars from kits sent from other Comecon countries. A number of joint ventures were recently set up to address the industry's shortcomings.

In May 1992, Rover announced that an agreement had been reached with the Ministry of Defence to transform a state-owned armaments company into a plant to produce Maestro cars and vans. Rover's initial investment was reported to be US$20 million rising to US$120 million as assembly lines would be introduced. Production was expected to start at 7000 units rising to 50,000 units within 5 years. Engines for the cars were to be supplied by Vamo, which already assembles engines under licence from Perkins of Great Britain.

Foreign interest in Bulgaria has recently developed in the electronics, chemical, steel and telecom sectors. A number of firms are in the process of investing in Bulgaria's communication technologies. US-based Sprint Corp, which is currently building Russia's first nationwide public data network to connect major cities, is also reported to have expressed a strong interest in building a national data network. With an average for the country of 30 telephones per 100 people, the telephone network needs substantial investment. In July 1992, foreign companies were invited to submit tenders for a US$230 million project to digitalise trunk and international telephone lines. Several Western companies showed an interest. The digitalisation programme is intended as the first phase of more thorough modernisation.

Among the main areas in which the Bulgarian government is keen on attracting foreign investors are the transport sectors (particularly the development of roads from Sofia to the Black Sea ports), and the upgrading of the Sofia airport. One additional area which has been identified as a key priority for foreign investment is environmental protection. Assistance has already been provided by supranational agencies and the European Community. Issues to be addressed range from reducing land and water pollution to clean energy. Bulgaria's rivers have already attracted attention from the Finnish group, Rauma Ecoplanning.

Energy-related infrastructure is among the sectors in which foreign investment is most needed. Bulgaria is still very dependent on the ex-Soviet Union for its oil and gas. Its electricity supply, most of which is assured by nuclear energy, is subject to frequent disruptions. Nuclear plants were developed under the communist regime and substantial overhauls are needed today. As a first step towards addressing a potential environmental hazard problem, a contract was recently awarded to Westinghouse of the US to construct a radioactive waste recycling plant at a cost of US$11 million.

A major private joint venture was recently set up between Environmental Oil Resources Inc (Enviroil) and the giant oil refinery Neftochim. Over a period of five years, Enviroil will reclaim the stagnant oil of Bulgaria's large lagoons and sell it to Neftochim at the prevailing world market price. The project is seen as an important pilot case for similar projects in Bulgaria and in Eastern Europe. Although the scheme's feasibility study was financed by the Know-How Fund, no support or guarantee was awarded from ECGD or any other source. The risks were entirely assumed by the private venture, which was reported to be pleasantly surprised at the speed, efficiency and enthusiasm with which their proposal was evaluated.

SOURCES OF FINANCE

Following Bulgaria's declaration of a moratorium on servicing its commercial bank and official indebtedness in March 1990, access to finance from Western commercial banks and export credit agencies was cut off. This had serious consequences for Bulgaria, reducing its ability to finance imports and cutting GDP. In the period after the moratorium, multilateral sources of finance were the main form of external funding available. During this period, the forms of finance discussed in the following five sections were made available to Bulgaria.

International institutions

After the IMF approval of a stand-by loan in February 1991 (which was finally disbursed in February 1992), a US$250 million credit line was opened by the World Bank to support the structural adjustment process. Several United Nations agencies (the United Nations Industrial Development Organisation, the Food and Agriculture Organisation and the United Nations Development Programme) also unblocked funds for specific projects involving technical assistance. The World Bank also made sector loans available, such as the recently announced US$75 million loan for the energy sector to be disbursed by March 1993.

Bulgaria is eligible for equity financing from the International Finance Corporation ('IFC'), which is prepared to take substantial minority equity stakes (up to 30 per cent) in projects.

Regional organisations

- The European Bank for Reconstruction and Development (EBRD), a London-based bank set up to assist Eastern European economies, became involved in Bulgaria in early-1991. A credit line was opened and extended to ECU90 million in early-1992. Examples of EBRD involvement include an ECU40 million loan granted in June 1992 for the extension of a coal power station in southern Bulgaria, in order to introduce clean technology and recycle waste efficiently.

- The European Investment Bank (EIB) invests in projects through co-financings. As an example, the EIB and the Bulgarian National Electricity Company co-financed the remainder of the above-mentioned project for ECU114 million.

- In 1991 the EC granted ECU290 million for restructuring the economy and boosting hard currency reserves.

- The US Agency for International Development provided US$10 million at the end of 1991.

- The EC Polish and Hungarian Assistance for the Reconstruction of Europe (PHARE) programme was extended to Bulgaria in 1991, having operated in most Eastern European countries. Bulgaria was allocated a US$200 million funding line over 2 years, of which 40 per cent was designated for privatisations, 25 per cent for agriculture modernisation, 20 per cent for health care and 10 per cent for the environment. Financing from PHARE is usually granted as a result of a bidding process.

- The Know-How Fund provides assistance to potential investors in Bulgaria. Companies registered and carrying on business in the United Kingdom, the Isle of Man or the Channel Islands may be able to look to this Fund for up to 50 per cent of the costs of a pre-investment feasibility study or for financing management training for prospective joint ventures. In both cases, the funding is discretionary and subject to a limit of £50,000 per application. Assistance may also be available for training and advice in the environmental sector. In addition, the Know-How Fund provides financial support for technical assistance projects in privatisations, the financial services and energy areas (priority sectors), and tourism, management education and public administration.

- The Bulgarian-American Enterprise Fund is a private, non-profit organisation which invests primarily in the food and agribusiness sectors. The fund makes loans, grants, and equity investments in addition to sponsoring technical assistance and training. The Bulgarian-American Enterprise Fund has approximately US$55 million available for investment and technical assistance over three years.

Export credit agencies

In the period following Bulgaria's agreement, in May 1991, of a restructuring of its Paris Club debt, a number of Western credit agencies extended lines to Bulgaria. For example, Hermes of Germany agreed on a DM50 million credit guarantee and Eximbank of Japan on a US$100 million loan. Once the first bilateral trade accord was signed between the USA and Bulgaria in April 1991, loans, investments and trade deals became eligible for government guarantees. However, a majority of Western agencies still do not provide medium-term cover, including the French COFACE and the British Export Credit Guarantee Department (ECGD).

Commercial banks

Due to the continuing failure to reach agreement with commercial bank creditors, Bulgaria has not been able to secure a resumption of commercial lending, and particularly of the short-term trade finance on which the country is dependent to fund imports. Access to new commercial bank funding is therefore likely to be determined by the outcome of negotiations between Bulgaria and its commercial creditors.

Funds

The Emerging Eastern European Fund was launched in October 1989 as the first fund for equity investment in Eastern Europe. It raised approximately US$50 million from private investors with an interest in direct involvement in Eastern European projects and approximately US$200 million from banks interested in swapping their loans to Eastern Europe for shares in the fund. The role of the fund managers was defined as providing both financial assistance and business expertise. Since 1990 a number of regional funds have been considering investing in Bulgaria. Whereas their main objective was initially to invest in Western European companies seeking opportunities to expand in Eastern Europe, an increasing feature of these funds' policy is to become involved in ventures through direct investment in local companies.

Part IV

Case Studies

Case Study 1

British Gas Exploration and Production

Report of an interview with Peter Schwarz, British Gas exploration manager for the UK and Europe

In the autumn of 1990, Bulgaria became the first country in Eastern Europe to open its borders to foreign participation in the search for oil and gas. Faced with a shortage of hard currency, a substantial foreign debt and a desire to become self sufficient in oil and gas, the Bulgarian government was prompted to seek foreign investment and participation in the search for new reserves.

There has been relatively little exploration in Bulgaria compared with its east European neighbours and as a consequence existing production levels were low. A total of 2.1 million barrels of oil and 135 million cubic metres of gas are produced each year, equating to a day's production in the North Sea. Over 97 per cent of the country's oil and gas is imported from the former Soviet Union and the Middle East.

In early 1990 the former Soviet Union announced its intention to end barter arrangements with its Comecon partners and indicated that in future all supplies would have to be paid for in hard currency at world market rates. As early as August 1989 the government drew up a strategy for hydrocarbon exploration and announced its first ever formal licence round in November of the same year. This proved to be a similar process to that adopted for the United Kingdom Continental Shelf and internationally. Applications were invited in June 1990 for ten tracts onshore and seven offshore along the margins of the Black Sea.

As part of a regional geological study of Eastern Europe, British Gas had highlighted Bulgaria as a country offering significant oil and gas potential, although some doubts were expressed about continued political and commercial stability. British Gas was attracted to Bulgaria not only because of the prospect of significant untapped reserves, but also as a consequence of the growing perception throughout Eastern Europe that gas would progressively replace oil and coal as the green fuel of the future.

In order to fully assess the hydrocarbon prospectivity of the country, British Gas purchased in excess of 14,000 kilometres of seismic data. These data were marketed by a small and independent seismic company on behalf of the Bulgarian State Committee of Geology and were interpreted by British Gas technical staff. As a result of their positive recommendation, British Gas submitted bids for one block offshore in the Black Sea and one onshore block adjacent to the city of Burgas.

Geographically, Bulgaria is situated at the crossroads between Europe, Asia and the Middle East. Geologically it is dominated by the Alpine Balkan mountain chain which extends from east to west across its borders. The formation of these mountains, caused by the collision of Africa and Asia 25 million years ago, was responsible for the development of complex structures which extend offshore under the thick Tertiary sediments of the Black Sea basin. In places, these sediments are 14–20 kilometres in thickness.

The Black Sea coast is an area of outstanding natural beauty and consequently of particular environmental sensitivity. It was therefore necessary to include within the application a detailed explanation of the Company's policy towards protecting the environment, as well as contingency plans to be adopted in the unlikely event of an oil spillage.

Following submission of its application, British Gas was invited to discuss its proposals with the Bulgarian State Committee of Geology in Varna, on the Black Sea Coast. This involved making a full presentation of the Company's technical capabilities and activities both in the United Kingdom and elsewhere in the world, and outlining the Company's intended seismic acquisition and drilling plans in Bulgaria. The meeting was attended by a number of geologists, geophysicists and engineers from the Committee of Geology, together with specialists from various academies and institutes. There were also local government representatives from the Black Sea area and members of the Green political parties who were particularly interested in the Company's proposed activities and its policies towards the environment.

The discussions were held in a semi-formal atmosphere and at all times were extremely friendly and good humoured with much patience being shown by both sides during the inevitably prolonged translation of some of the more difficult issues. It was immediately evident that the Bulgarians possessed considerable expertise in the technical aspects of the oil and gas exploration and production business, as many of their specialists had worked outside the country, although their experience of the western commercial side of the industry was less well developed. The Bulgarians were, and continue to be, particularly hospitable and at all times endeavoured to accommodate the wishes of their guests.

Against strong competition from major European and American companies, British Gas was awarded the Kamchia block (Block IV) in the Black Sea and the onshore Burgas block (Block 10), centred on the coastal city of Burgas (illustrated in the map below).

The Kamchia block was the most promising area of those awarded. Two wells had been drilled during the 1980s with modest amounts of gas being tested from a number of hydrocarbon bearing intervals. Several structures having the capacity to hold substantial reserves of gas or oil had been identified on the licence. These prospects will be

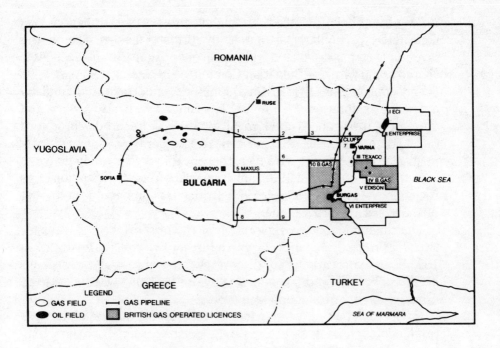

Map 1 *Licence status and infrastructure*

drilled during the initial five-year exploration period of the licence.

Onshore, Block 10 looked particularly interesting in terms of its regional geological setting although several exploration wells drilled previously in the area had failed to discover any economic oil or gas reserves.

The awards were made, as in the United Kingdom, against the applicant fulfilling certain criteria. These were:

- work programme for each block;

- technical competence;

- financial strength;

- international exploration experience;

- contribution to the Bulgarian economy;

- technology transfer;

- training of Bulgarian personnel;

- consideration of the environment.

As well as being viewed as highly prospective, Bulgaria was considered particularly attractive by British Gas because of the favourable terms associated with the licence. Equity in the licences is shared 50:50 with the Bulgarian Committee of Geology. As part of its licence obligations, British Gas agreed to undertake and fund an extensive exploration programme. The company will also pay a rental on each of the licences and a royalty on any hydrocarbons produced on a sliding scale from 12.5 per cent to 17.5 per cent. To assist early payback of the project, however, there is a five-year tax holiday.

In the first quarter of 1992, only two years from the initiation of its regional evaluation in March 1990, British Gas embarked on its first offshore seismic programme.

The timetable for the exploration of the offshore licence calls for two wells to be drilled in 1993 with a further two wells to be drilled in 1994/95. If hydrocarbons are discovered, after appraisal, a decision is likely to be taken on commerciality in 1995/96, with a view to bringing on any production by 1998/99.

No decision has yet been made on the eventual market for any gas produced. It could go directly into the domestic market or there may be opportunities to export to neighbouring countries.

Although British Gas is not currently planning to become involved in the downstream hydrocarbon business, it is possible that opportunities might present themselves in power generation and distribution.

To support its activities in Bulgaria, British Gas opened an office in Sofia in September 1990 and now has a team of six British and American expatriates and six Bulgarian national personnel in place. The Sofia office is supplemented by a small operational office and shore base in the Black Sea resort town of Varna.

As one of its licence commitments British Gas has undertaken to finance the training of Bulgarian personnel and a portion of its annual budget is set aside for this purpose. The Committee of Geology has also agreed to second members of its staff into the British Gas organisation so that they can become familiar with the latest techniques used in the exploration for and production of hydro-carbons, as well as becoming familiar with the Company's procedures and working practices.

During its three-year association with Bulgaria, British Gas has encountered a number of challenges, some of which are listed below:

- Historically, neither Bulgarians nor Western Europeans have had many opportunities to study each other's languages, so the services of translators and interpreters are essential.

- Bulgarians are by nature extremely polite and will not disagree with a guest. This can lead to misunderstandings.

- In Eastern Europe, negotiating and conducting business progresses less quickly than in the West.

- Information which would be considered common knowledge in the West may be difficult to obtain in Bulgaria. For example, because of military and security restrictions, British Gas found it impossible to obtain topographic maps and satellite images of the country. Both of these are essential for onshore exploration.

- Most specialist equipment has to be imported.

- The expatriate community is small and there are shortages of some foodstuffs and consumer items. This makes it a challenging overseas assignment for employees.

- The business infrastructure within the country is not well established.

However, considerable progress is being made in overcoming these difficulties, and any obstacles are more than outweighed by the many advantages of conducting business in Bulgaria. These include:

- Realistic business expectations among the various government authorities, who have set taxes and benefits at levels which encourage foreign investment.

- Relatively stable political situation.

- Friendly people who are enthusiastic about investment in their country.

- An extremely high standard of education.

- A strong work ethic.

- Relatively inexpensive operating costs.

- Good transport infrastructure.

- Low crime rate.

- Good climate.

Looking forward to the future, British Gas maintains a firm belief that Bulgaria is a country which offers both significant opportunity and a potentially stable political and commercial climate in which to develop its business. However, it also recognises that the country faces a period of great uncertainty during its transformation to a full market economy and that a number of obstacles will have to be overcome before its aspirations are realised.

Domaine Boyar

Report of an interview with Margarit Todorov, managing director of Domaine Boyar

As managing director of Bulgarian Vintners during the 1980s, Margarit Todorov was instrumental in establishing Bulgarian wine as a major force in the British market in the 80s. He is now seeking to build on that success with his own company, Domaine Boyar, as well as developing the drinks market in Bulgaria itself as exclusive distributor for United Distillers.

Bulgaria's wine industry was developed intensively from the 1960s onwards as a specialised part of Comecon. An honest, alcoholic red wine was produced which was drunk all over the old Soviet bloc. It was 'heavy enough to carry in your handkerchief!' For consumers it was a matter of drinking to get drunk, not of enjoying the taste.

In the late 1970s the government decided to concentrate on sales for hard currency through Vinprom, the state monopoly trading organisation concerned with wine. The organisation was blessed with university educated growers with good technical skills and a marketing philosophy that it was not a question of whether the wine was good or bad, but whether it could be sold in the West or not. That lead towards efforts to improve and adapt attributes such as flavour, fragrance and body.

MARKETING STRATEGY

The UK was the main market targeted, as it is the largest non-wine growing importer in the world. The absence of a local industry also means that consumers are much more open to new labels. Vinprom did not seek to take on the established market leaders from France and Italy, but to compete in the mass market with other East

Europeans. In the late 1970s the critical price was £1.99 or under (about £3 today), which represented 70 per cent of the market.

Whilst Bulgaria certainly enjoyed cost advantages through subsidies and managed prices, there were significant production costs (such as bottling and labelling) involved in producing for the West.

A combination of luck and good strategy lay behind the huge sales growth of Bulgarian wine in the 1980s. The luck was the discovery of Bulgarian Cabernet Sauvignon by Hugh Johnson for the *Sunday Times* Wine Club. The strategy was the establishment of Bulgarian Vintners in 1980 and the development of a more coherent marketing strategy. At the time, German Liebfraumilch dominated the market and the wine trade was neglecting the potential for red. Bulgarian Vintners anticipated that the newcomers to wine that Liebfraumilch had brought into the market would graduate from sweet to dry white and then to red. This process was hastened by the advent of the California wines which did a great deal to educate the British consumer in recognising the wine grape varieties. The subsequent rise of the dollar left great gaps in the market to be exploited.

During the 1970s, 30,000 cases of Bulgarian wine were being sold each year. This had risen to 70,000 by 1982, mainly through the *Sunday Times* and Peter Dominic. A new policy was then adopted by Bulgarian Vintners of offering wines across the whole range, backed up with a campaign to win over suppliers and connoisseurs. This resulted in sales of a million cases a year by 1986 – nearly the same as Portugal.

Market research showed that this total was primarily made up of regular drinkers; others would not touch the product because of a prejudice against Bulgaria *per se*. A TV advertising campaign in 1986 tackled this head on: guests at a smart dinner party are flabbergasted to find that the delightful wine they are drinking is in fact Bulgarian. Sales subsequently exploded. By 1988, Bulgarian Vintners were selling two million cases a year and were the third largest supplier of red wines, behind the French and the Italians.

The UK not only represented the biggest export market for Bulgarian wine by far, but also the most profitable. The proceeds were invested in improving production and packaging creating an upward spiral of quality for the wine industry overall. Margarit Todorov argues that the Bulgarian wine industry is now the most advanced in Eastern Europe. It is no longer a matter of individual cultivation but of mass production.

Wineries were originally set up in the 1960s close to big towns, while two wineries were chosen in the late 1970s purely for markets in the West. By the mid 1980s the flow of foreign exchange earnings allowed others to become progressively more specialised. Typically, small export wineries were set up as units within larger facilities and there are now 20 to 30 export wineries scattered all over the country.

The production monopoly of Vinprom was dismantled in November 1990, making each winery an independent unit. Many are still state owned, but a restitution law at the beginning of 1992 meant that those run as co-operatives before 1947 could be returned to their original owners.

The wineries are well placed in terms of facilities and have a limited need for new investment. Viticulture is the area where there is a more urgent need for improvement. The restitution law has meant that these properties also have been, by and large, returned to private owners.

It is important for the Bulgarian wine industry to increase its sales to the West, not only to generate hard currency earnings but also to overcome the collapse of its former markets in Comecon. These have been in severe decline since 1984 when President Gorbachev started his campaign against alcohol in the Soviet Union. That year, Bulgaria sold 30 million cases (380 million bottles) to the Soviet Union. Six years later, this was down to only 10 per cent of that level. Vineyards were uprooted or neglected altogether.

BATTLING FOR MARKET SHARE

One of the companies to emerge from the fragmentation of the wine monopoly was Vinimpex, the export company that virtually owned Bulgarian Vintners in the UK. What they tried to do was to secure its monopoly in the UK by giving each winery a share of the market. It was a policy with which Margarit Todorov disagreed. In his view, competition was inevitable. He resigned as managing director of Bulgarian Vintners and set up a new Bulgarian wine distributor – Domaine Boyar – which is acting for four wineries, including Suhindol, the main export area since the 1970s. He regrets that a 'mega battle for market share' is now taking place. The result is that sales of quality wine are falling. In 1991, the lower range country wine accounted for 30 per cent of the UK market, the medium range for 50 per cent and the premium brand for 20 per cent. By 1992, these proportions had changed to 60 per cent, 30 per cent and 5 per cent respectively.

Domaine Boyar started trading in 1992 and is aiming for a 30 per cent share of the market in 1993. The main focus of Margarit Todorov's activities at present has been to develop Rosim & Co, an exclusive distributorship for United Distillers in Bulgaria.

Scotch whisky is by far the most prestigious drink for Bulgarians and accounts for 70 per cent to 80 per cent of the imported spirits market. Johnnie Walker has a 50 per cent share of Scotch whisky sales. The luxury spirits market is concentrated in Sofia which accounts for half of total sales. Rosim & Co runs the most prestigious shops anywhere in Bulgaria, which not only sells whisky but also Swiss watches such as Cartier and Longines. As well as being sold in virtually all good shops and duty free shops, the other main outlets for United Distillers products are nightclubs, restaurants and tourist resorts.

Whatever the political or economic climate, whisky sales have been remarkably consistent in Bulgaria. In the long term there is the potential for growth. Margarit Todorov estimates that about 10 per cent to 15 per cent of the population has discretionary spending power and this is increasing year by year.

High taxation is creating havoc in the market. A legally imported bottle of Scotch with all duties paid would cost in excess of £20 a bottle. The effect of this has been to create an enormous black market in whisky and other spirits to avoid paying excise, with the result that the government is receiving next to nothing in revenue.

Overall it is a harsh business climate. Interest rates are at 50 per cent and industry is at a standstill. Managers are inexperienced and have no sense of business ethics or practice. Restructuring is by a process of cut-throat competition. Margarit Todorov's underlying faith in the market springs from a perception that in five years things will start to lift off and that Bulgarians are well educated with a greater ability than their counterparts in the West to turn their hands to most things.

Case Study 3

ICL

Report of an interview with Rod Allen, ICL's sales manager, Central Europe

ICL, one of Europe's leading information systems companies, has had a presence in Bulgaria since 1968, although over the last three years the nature of its activities has fundamentally changed.

After the fall of the communist regime, business took a severe downturn, although this soon improved in 1991 with sales of £1.8 million and 1992 targets were exceeded by April. None the less, ICL will continue to look at Bulgaria as a developing market until it achieves annual sales of £3 million to £4 million. That should be achievable once economic aid from the EC and the World Bank starts flowing.

ICL's business developed rapidly throughout the region in the late 1960s and early 1970s. Political and financial constraints triggered the closure of its Sofia office in 1975, but the company re-entered the market in a serious way in 1980 and ran a technical co-operation arrangement until 1989 with a partner from the Bulgarian Academy of Sciences. In reality this was a thinly disguised agent, providing ICL with sales leads as well as carrying spare parts.

ICL was principally involved in selling mainframe office systems to government organisations and commercial sales were limited. The emphasis was on selling hardware because the Bulgarians specialised in electronics within Comecon and had a number of very large software houses with up to 2000 employees. This meant that there was little interest in application software, customers held their own spare parts and carried out their own maintenance. Bulgaria was also a market heavily restricted by the CoCom regime, designed to prevent the transfer to the Soviet bloc of technology which might be put to a military use.

THE NEW MARKET-PLACE

The political transformation of Bulgaria brought about a complete
change in the market for IT products. The bottom dropped out of
existing markets and business was depressed for about 12 to 18
months. Consumer profiles underwent a radical alteration and in
terms of products the Bulgarians have 'gone crazy' for PCs. More
enlightened organisations are now looking for total solutions,
including application package software, maintenance and project
management. Indeed they are using such systems as an agent for the
change to a market economy.

The competition for business is 'breathtaking'. At a rough estimate,
IBM has 30 per cent of the market, Taiwanese clones have 30 per
cent, ICL has 10 per cent with the rest split between smaller
suppliers. Grey imports and the distortions created by CoCom still
make it difficult to judge the size of the market.

The service element of ICL's business is now developing rapidly. A
full spares and service operation has been set up: in 1990 no service
revenue was generated; in 1992 it should reach £70,000; and by 1993
it is projected at £200,000.

ICL made an unsuccessful attempt to set up a joint venture with its
former partners, preferring in the end to deal directly. A company as
dominant as IBM may be able to control relations with agents and
distributors, but for smaller suppliers these relationships may not be
as easy to control.

The first sector to open up was banking. ICL won the contract with
the State Savings Bank to supply the hardware for an internal
banking system. Tourism, especially hotels, will be looking to upgrade
facilities and, with an eye to the future, ICL is monitoring the drastic
process of restructuring in manufacturing.

The level of business from Western investors is limited at the
moment, although ICL has contracts with three British multi-
nationals. They place considerable value on the level of service ICL
is able to offer. By contrast, price is still all important for Bulgarian
customers and ICL finds itself trading on paper-thin margins. In a
competitive market, full of cheap or even non-functioning PCs, prices
are unbundled to reflect commodity basics.

While service is recognised as a significant benefit it is not
something that Bulgarians are accustomed to paying for. Instead they
turn to small local organisations which can be retained for as little as
£2 per month, which may look cheap until it is time to buy in spare
parts.

Marketing is relatively underdeveloped in the conduct of day-to-day business. Given £5000 and a choice between taking on another salesman or carrying out some promotional activity, the former would be the choice of most.

TRANSACTING BUSINESS

Economic circumstances mean that there are some particular points of emphasis in negotiating contracts with potential customers. Questions such as advance payments, bank guarantees and performance guarantees demand a degree of flexibility.

It is difficult to establish the credit standing of companies, so ICL tends to ask for 100 per cent cash in advance. Bulgarians often prefer this to the cost of a letter of credit. One offer that ICL makes is to take the money and put it in a deposit account, drawing money as it becomes due and in the mean time paying interest to the Bulgarian customer. It is an idea that can seem too good to be true when it is first presented and Bulgarians need some convincing that they are not being taken for a ride. ICL only does a small proportion of its business in leva – sufficient to cover local costs.

The style of negotiations is becoming increasingly simple and direct. The priority now is to make things happen as quickly as possible. ICL recently concluded a major contract in three-and-a-half days which could have taken weeks under the old regime.

There are three riders to this improvement in business transactions. Gaps in the understanding of often basic business assumptions can cause difficulties. 'If after an hour of discussions, you find that you are not getting through, go back to the beginning. The difficulty often springs from a term which the Bulgarians profess to understand, but to which they assign a quite different meaning from you,' comments Rod Allen. One ICL deal was threatened for several weeks because the Bulgarian party did not appreciate the difference between retail price and profit.

The second rider is the growing unpredictability in the award of business. The third is the need to be extremely wary of private companies, many of which are not adequately financed or managed, and have an alarming habit of collapsing overnight.

Nor do Bulgarians 'buy into' the Western concept of training as there is a tendency to believe it is all for show and as a result people may revert to normal. Changing the feel of an organisation is hard work. Management is either laid back or authoritarian. Neither fits

ICL's demand for self-reliant profit centres. Rod Allen cites one instance of the organisational difficulties. ICL was asked to instal a PC next morning for the managing director of a new Western investment. When chased up the following afternoon, the employee assigned to the task said that the secretary agreed that it was alright to go in on Monday!

ICL staff all speak English and are extremely well qualified technically. There seems to be a perception that there is a need for a PhD to do the job! This can lead to frustration as technical maintenance does not offer a sufficient intellectual challenge. These types of difficulties are being surmounted and, for ICL, persistence is bringing rewards.

Case Study 4

Racal Recorders

*Report of an interview with Graham Clark and David Briggs,
sales managers with responsibility for Bulgaria.*

The Bulgarian revolution at the end of 1989 'shot to pieces' the
strategies that Racal Recorders had been pursuing over several years
in that market. A completely new start had to be made. By 1991 this
was begining to show results, most significantly in the shape of an
order worth £300,000 from the Bulgarian air traffic authority.

Racal Recorders supply voice recorders for use where an
emergency situation or contractual obligations places heavy reliance
on the spoken word as evidence. Product capabilities range from a
single channel up to large systems that can record hundreds of
telephone or radio lines.

In Eastern Europe it used to be possible to pay lip service to
demands for health and safety, but reintegration into the world
economy requires the rigorous adoption of standards. In eastern
Germany this is happening very quickly and a wide range of business
opportunities are opening up in emergency services. This process is
happening more slowly in Bulgaria, although it has none the less
become Racal's second largest market in the region after Poland.

A further boost to the potential for Racal's products might have
been expected from the lifting of CoCom restrictions on sales of
technology with any kind of military application. Demand for the
more technologically advanced of Racal's range however is limited. In
any case, licensing imports to the market is still complicated,
especially in an area as sensitive as electronics.

THE AIR TRAFFIC CONTRACT

Improving airport facilities was a major priority for Bulgaria, as it is integral to increasing trade and foreign exchange earnings. In 1991, Racal Recorders won an order worth £300,000 to supply the Bulgarian Air Traffic Services Authority with a multi-channel, voice logger ICR 64, for recording ground-to-air communications as well as digital weather information.

Racal was in a stronger position to win the order than its four main Western rivals by virtue of having had a presence in the market for 20 years. The Bulgarian customer's main concern was on the technical side and Racal built up a rapport through visits, site surveys and system design. Being able to talk to a Western company means a great deal to the Bulgarians.

One of the main contractual concerns was with warranties. What happened if the system broke down? It was an important part of the deal that Racal was able to provide the back-up of trained engineers through its agency, with a commitment to send someone over from the UK as necessary. Equal emphasis was placed on certifying the quality of the equipment.

Finance was relatively straightforward as the order was for an international airport. Racal is being paid out of the flow of hard currency earnings generated from landing and airspace fees.

EMERGENCY SERVICES AND THE COMMERCIAL SECTOR

Racal is developing prospects in the emergency services through demonstrations and exhibitions, such as the Plovdiv Fair. More and more authorities and companies are coming on to the market with their own budgets, although these are small at the moment. Racal's attitude is that operating in Bulgaria is like working in a recession in the UK. Products need to be kept to the fore in preparation for when the economic cycle turns up.

For the present, there is very little money, which means that it is important to choose customers carefully – usually those dealing with the West. Racal has not yet benefited from aid-related funds.

The market for voice recording in the commercial sector is still limited. All the same, this is worth targeting, particularly in areas such as banking, because liberalisation means that people are increasingly being made responsible for their own decisions.

In terms of doing business, the old ways under central planning may have been slow and inefficient but were at least relatively clear and predictable. It is not easy now to find the right person to talk to about business and end-users are inexperienced in negotiating contracts and making financial arrangements. This environment necessitates some form of presence in Bulgaria to nurse potential customers. Racal opened a representative office two years ago. This is staffed by a local agent 'who is as enthusiastic as a Jack Russell' and learning rapidly about contracts.

The agent is not yet ready to become a full-blown distributor and Bulgarians are in any case much more willing to buy from the West than from East Europeans. Racal executives from the UK fly in and out all the time to support business development and to provide technical advice.

The tendency is for Western companies to enter the market without acquiring specialist management skills. It is not possible just to go in and find an agent. There is a need for thorough groundwork followed up with technical and management support. Investment and eduction go hand-in-hand.

Racal sees a limit to the risks of operating in Bulgaria. Whatever complexion a government may have, international trade is going to be one of its main priorities. On the positive side, 'things are changing at a rate of knots and foreign exchange is having a strong multiplier effect. It's an environment where you have to be fast on your feet!'

Appendices

Appendix 1

Opportunities by Sector

Cerrex Ltd

ENERGY

Coal (60 per cent), mainly imported from the former USSR, and nuclear power (over 30 per cent) supply almost all Bulgaria's power requirements.

In total, indigenous energy resources supply about one-third of the country's requirements. The country has little natural gas and few gas pipelines, and hydroelectricity, in spite of ambitious plans, remains relatively unimportant. Oil reserves are still commercially insignificant but will probably gain in importance: in October 1991 leading companies (Texaco, Enterprise Oil, OMV of Austria and British Gas) obtained concessions on the Black Sea shelf and in eastern Bulgaria for oil and gas prospecting, and other companies have been prospecting for a number of years. Locally mined coal is of low calorific value and insufficient for the country's needs, although it is used in power generation at thermal power stations situated at Maritsa Iztok and at Varna.

Since the first nuclear reactor was opened in Kozlodui in north-west Bulgaria in the late-1960s, nuclear power has contributed an increasing proportion – in 1990 some 14,000 million kilowatt-hours or over 30 per cent of the country's energy requirements. The two oldest 440 kilowatt reactors were shut down temporarily at the end of 1991 for refurbishment, removing 15 per cent of Bulgaria's power from the grid. Plans to increase nuclear capacity in order to reduce dependency on imported coal have met increasing opposition on environmental grounds.

Bulgaria none the less has to face the fact that it will need to pay a more commercial rate in hard currency for its energy in the future, and this sector is expected to provide very major opportunities for

UK industry. Unless the country can develop a guaranteed source of energy at a reasonable price, it will find increasing difficulty in achieving production targets, maintaining exports and converting to a more Western orientated economy. Energy is expected to take a large part of Bulgaria's national resources and foreign aid, including PHARE, EIB and the World Bank.

The country has for several years been running an energy saving programme. Plans introduced in 1984 and 1989 had as their aims the 5 per cent annual decrease of energy usage – targets of 2.6 per cent were set for the textile industry and 6 per cent for metallurgy – to increase from 15 per cent to 35 per cent the proportion of buildings with piped heating, and to give families access to local heating grids.

The country's first requirement has been to secure the safety of the nuclear production capacities but major priorities will be the improvement of fuel and energy production and utilisation, the development of alternative sources of energy, conversion of present nuclear and fossil fuel generation to other forms (hydroelectricity and gas are the most likely) and the introduction of energy saving measures for both domestic and industrial usage. Under the PHARE programme, ECU15 million and ECU11 million have been granted to bring Bulgaria's power stations into line with international operation and safety standards. Assistance will also be aimed at replacing and modernising generating facilities, reducing emissions, more economic use of energy resources, the planning of tariffs more orientated towards supply and demand and bringing in more skilled staff for the operation of power stations.

AGRICULTURE AND FOOD PROCESSING

This area's traditional strengths in the export market and in agricultural research, the introduction of aid from the major donors and the sector as a major employer will make it an area of high priority and good opportunities.

Total agricultural production has fallen by about 10 per cent in the past decade (vegetables, wine and tobacco have all fallen) although production of wheat (replacing maize) and some livestock (excluding poultry and sheep) has increased and, during the past year, certain surpluses have been available for export. The overall decline can be attributed in part to a series of successive droughts, insufficient priority under previous five-year plans and, more recently, uncertainty over the implementation of the land restitution laws. Previous policies will now be reversed and agriculture is expected to be encouraged. (One-sixth of the population are now involved in agriculture compared to four-fifths some 40 years ago.)

Several companies including Bayer, Hoechst, BASF and Schering have shown confidence in the future by increasing their presence in Bulgaria in the area of fertilisers and pesticides. The World Bank has offered a credit of some $50 million for this industry including, among other items, privatisation of food processing enterprises, and this is part of an internationally funded agricultural development project of about $110 million agreed in the middle of 1992. The EC have given ECU14.3 million in maize, potato and tomato seed, together with technical aid for Bulgarian agriculture, including an allocation under the PHARE programme for veterinary products.

In 1990, food processing represented 22 per cent of total industrial output and accounted for a major portion of Bulgarian exports. The industry consisted of over 600 enterprises (some of which have modern automated machinery) and employed 168,000 people. Production included vegetable and edible oils, preserves, canned fruit and vegetables, confectionery, beer and soft drinks – many of excellent quality – meat and meat products and dairy products. Major markets were the Soviet Union and other Eastern European countries.

Although the industry has generally suffered from a lack of investment, there are notable exceptions. New and modernised enterprises making soft drinks, sauces, baby foods, vegetable oils, bread and pastry products, and a large milling combine in Sofia have been set up. The results of investment have shown through, *inter alia*, in the increase in production of meat products and beer. A start has been made in the manufacture of ready-to-serve foods, dietetic products, fruit juices and concentrates and new types of cheeses, meat and delicatessen.

Bulgaria has only been able to supply about one-quarter of the machinery required for the food processing and packaging industry, and there is need for modern processing, packaging, canning and deep freezing equipment, together with the production of a wide variety of glass bottles, jars, paper, polyethylene and PVC packaging materials for the domestic and export markets. In the past, most food processing and packaging machinery was supplied by Eastern European manufacturers, plus some from Italy and Germany but, in future, Bulgaria must look more towards the West and will be seeking technical co-operation agreements and partnerships, licence deals and buy-back.

WINE

Commercial wine production started in Bulgaria in the 1960s and was mostly for export to the Soviet Union and other East European countries. In 1979, Bulgarian wines were first exported outside the Eastern bloc to Japan and Canada, followed a year or so later by exports to the UK and the USA. They have since diversified their ranges and become well established.

Bulgarian winemaking establishments are reasonably well equipped with up-to-date machinery and technology. The industry is still, however, suffering from the reorientation that resulted from the anti-alcohol campaign in the Soviet Union in 1985 when, through the loss of this important market, the Bulgarian grape growers destroyed many vines and failed to replant. Investment in vineyards was neglected and Bulgaria lost much export income. In 1985, Bulgarian exports of wine totalled 211 million litres of which 135 million litres was sold to the Soviet Union, with only minimal exports to the West. By 1990 total exports had fallen by half and those to the former USSR were only 25 million litres. Increased sales to the West (in particular the UK – one of the success stories of the Bulgarian economy) could not make up for the shortfall.

Prior to November 1990, the Bulgarian wine industry consisted of 4 regional companies, the main one representing 80 per cent of output and controlled from Sofia. The new system comprises over 40 separate companies established under the aegis of the Union of Wine Producers of Bulgaria which was set up to ensure that quality is maintained and to encourage research and development. When privatised, vine growing and vineries should both benefit from being under joint management.

The main requirements appear to be investment in vine planting stock, plant protection chemicals, up-to-date bottling and processing equipment, and multi-functional picking and sorting machinery. Present indications are that investment in these areas could easily be recouped bearing in mind the sector's potential world-wide market, the high quality of its product and the marketing expertise presently available.

TOBACCO

Tobacco and cigarettes account for 50 per cent of Bulgaria's exported agriculture and processed agricultural products. Some 80 per cent of its annual cigarette output (about 90 million pieces) was traditionally exported. The Bulgarian tobacco industry has entered into a wide range of co-operation agreements with major tobacco companies in Germany, the USA, Switzerland and others, but to date there have been no joint ventures.

It has suffered from a decade of declining output accelerated by labour problems among Turkish workers and by the recent loss of major markets in the USSR and the Middle East. Efforts to stimulate increased production during 1991 resulted in increases in prices paid to farmers for their tobacco, but these increases were balanced by the rapid rise in the cost of supplies to farmers, while other crops can be grown more profitably on the same land.

Major opportunities will be in helping the Bulgarians to open up new markets (although this is hampered by the general decline in smoking in Western Europe and North America) and co-operation in cigarette production. Production of Oriental leaf has proved difficult to mechanise but alternatives include strain improvement, the production of aromatic elements and acceptable fertilisers and additives and technology in Virginia blend cigarettes. Once the question of an adequate supply of labour to produce the leaf is resolved, there are possibilities of developing cigar and pipe tobacco manufacture which could regain some lost sales and help extending their base in the duty-free market.

TOURISM

The Bulgarian tourist industry has developed over the past 25 years as a result of cheap package holidays from Eastern Europe to the Black Sea resorts. Until recently, of the 2 million tourists visiting Bulgaria over three-quarters were from the former Soviet Union and other Eastern European countries with under 80,000 from the UK. Although 1991 was a bad year for the Bulgarian tourist industry (with visitors from the UK down by 15 per cent and those from Eastern Europe by 90 per cent) this sector is expected to be one of the most promising for UK investment and as a currency earner for the Bulgarian economy. The great influx of Western tourists that the country might justifiably expect, the great variety that it has to offer, its cheapness for the tourist and low local overheads should guarantee high returns for investors.

At the end of the 1980s, Bulgaria started to create new facilities along the Black Sea coast – seaside resorts such as Albena, holiday villages or camps at Dyuni and Elenite and in the mountains with a holiday hotel accommodating 2000 at Borovets. Hotels in the main towns of Sofia (Rodina, Sheraton) and Plovdiv (Leningrad) were either built or substantially renovated usually in co-operation with Western companies. Development of numerous spas and mountain resorts (Sandanski) and ski centres at Borovets, Pamporovo and Bansko and specialist holidays (such as ornithology and hang-gliding) continue to take place.

The Bulgarian Committee for Tourism has estimated that US$8 billion is required for this industry. The sector will need to reorientate itself more to the requirements of Western tourists and develop infrastructure that can cope with far larger numbers than at present (eg improvement of its airports and roads, the introduction of amenities like motels, travel agencies, service stations, extra training, improved hotel management, booking software facilities, etc). Uncertainty will also continue to exist until the present problems of restitution and land ownership are sorted out.

The aims will be to upgrade and modernise many of the two star hotels to three or four star, build more four and five star hotels in the main towns (essentially for businessmen), construct higher class accommodation in the holiday villages, open up areas of natural beauty and of cultural or historic interest such as Pliska, Veliko Turnovo and Madara, to improve ski facilities and build recreation facilities such as golf courses. Privatisation of the sector will also throw up opportunities for Western investors with the transfer of restaurants, shops, hotels and tourist services to private interests.

CHEMICALS AND ALLIED TRADES

This sector represented 18.1 per cent of total production in 1980 but only 13.2 per cent in 1990. 110,000 people are employed in this sector, or 7.6 per cent of the total work force.

The Bulgarian chemical industry expanded rapidly throughout the 1970s and early-1980s but the impetus was lost in the second half of the decade and fell even more sharply in 1990–91, particularly in those areas dependent on oil such as the petrochemical industry. Bulgaria is self-sufficient in most basic chemicals and rubber products, including nitrogenous fertilisers, soda ash, oil-based fuels and lubricants, industrial plastics, detergents, and tyres. Bulgaria also produces much of its requirements of sulphuric acid, caustic soda, paints, pigments and chemical fibres. About 20 per cent of the output of this sector has been exported to Eastern Europe and the Middle East.

Areas where investment and growth are sought (parts of which could be covered by the PHARE programme, the World Bank and The European Bank) include agricultural chemicals and phosphatic fertilisers (Stara Zagora), PVC (Devnya), phthalic and maleic anhydride (Rousse), glucose, dextrine etc (Razgrad), cooking salt (Devnya), urea, polyethylene, ethylene (Bourgas), alkylbenzene (Yambol), benzaldehyde, methanol (Plovdiv) and viscous fibres (Svishtov). Other sectors are substances for microelectronics, optoelectronics, laser techniques, washing agents, paint, heavy lubricants, anti-corrosion, synthetic rubber and chemicals for the food industry.

Problems are increasingly occurring through old equipment, inefficient purification equipment, old technologies and lack of investment over a number of years, although some modernisation of the industry has taken place in the last few years with priority being given to improving production technologies, automation and the introduction of waste-free technologies.

Western companies already involved in agreements with Bulgarian companies include Montedison and ENI (Italy), Technip (France), Heinrich Koppers, Bayer and Hoechst (Germany), Taijin (Japan) and Occidental (USA). There is a proposed joint venture in this sector between Marc Rich and Neftochim to reconstruct and modernise a paraffin plant.

MEDICAL AND PHARMACEUTICALS SECTOR

In 1990 the number of doctors was 31.7 per thousand of population, dentists 6.8 per thousand and pharmacists 125 per thousand. There were 125 hospital beds per 10,000 persons, with 3747 out-patient establishments and 256 hospitals. In 1991, some Lev6 billion was spent on health care (5.2 per cent of GNP).

Private involvement is intended for the health service including modernisation of the system, restructuring and upgrading of hospitals, the introduction of a health insurance system and the import, production and distribution of medicines and medical equipment. Relations between the UK and Bulgarian medical authorities are good and the two countries have a co-operation agreement for information exchange covering the organisation of health services, education and training of staff, maternal and child health and disease prevention.

Aid already features highly in this sector. Assistance has been given for the delivery, distribution and sale of medicines and for mother and child care and there are proposals for a loan from the World Bank and a further fund of Lev60 million to assist in the health care system. A tentative $30 million programme for health care restructuring has been agreed. Under PHARE I, a total of ECU15 million has been distributed, ECU10 million for emergency medicine, ECU3.5 million for training of personnel, ECU0.5 million for technical assistance in drug policy and ECU1 million for health insurance.

The pharmaceutical industry's main products include human and animal antibiotics, natural and synthetic oils, toiletries and cosmetics, fine chemicals, medicine and drugs, and vitamins. Some 80 per cent of their turnover (about US$1 billion) has been exported through Pharmacim Co, to nearly 100 countries including the USSR (by far the largest), the USA, Japan, and Germany. Bulgaria has one of the world's largest pharmaceutical product ranges (over 1200 types of ready-made pharmaceuticals). It is the world's second largest manufacturer of veterinary microbial products and one of the industry's main strengths has been preparations for the treatment of cardio-vascular and intestinal conditions and antibiotics for nervous disorders. Classical antibiotics manufactured include cephalosporins, for which a new line is to be laid down in 1992 for Penicillin G-Raw, 7 ACK and, on the basis of these, new generations of cephalosporins are expected.

Because it is essentially a producer of mass drugs, the Bulgarian industry has been unable to take advantage of the movement towards generic drugs. The cost of research covering such a wide product range and the need to meet the high requirements for registration of exports to the EC and USA markets may present difficulties in selling ready-made pharmaceuticals to those markets and this may be one major area where Western investment and co-operation could help.

Six joint stock companies based around analgesic, vitamins and tonics (in Sofia), antibiotics, anti hypertension, drugs, cardio and tonic drugs (at Stanka Dimitrov), blood transfusion and infusion solutions (the Chemical and Pharmaceutical Research Institute) and sanitary and dressing materials (at Sandanski) have been established out of the previous state monopoly. These are already in discussions about industrial co-operation with French, Swiss, Italian and USA firms. Projects for mutual collaboration include plans to produce antibiotics (Razgrad and Rousse), enzymes (Botevgrad), vitamins

(Stanke Dimitrov), pharmaceuticals (Sofia), sanitary materials (Sandanski) and finished medicines and toothpaste (Plovdiv).

THE ENVIRONMENT

In the late-1980s, severe environmental difficulties caused by Bulgarian attempts at rapid industrialisation became an important political issue. Underpricing of energy and raw materials in Bulgaria had led to usage per unit substantially higher than in the West. An emphasis on generating energy from low quality brown coal together with outdated or inappropriate technologies in heavy industries (especially ferrous and non-ferrous, chemical and cement factories) and excessive application of fertilisers resulted in air pollution (mainly by sulphur dioxide and nitrogen oxide). Other problems include nitrate and manganese contamination of some of Bulgaria's underground river and water supplies, damage by untreated pollutants to considerable areas of the country's arable land and accumulation of industrial and household waste (an estimated 1000 tonnes per capita).

During 1990 and 1991, domestic resources available for this sector were spent mainly on the construction of water purification stations and equipment, and soil reclamation. The Sofia council is considering the introduction of environmental taxation and a special programme to use funds supplied by international institutions to help solve the city's environmental problems. None the less, an overall strategy is still needed to control and enforce standards and agree priorities. Money for monitoring air and water quality has been made available under the PHARE programme.

Equipment is needed for monitoring and improving the quality of the air, soil and water, together with hazardous waste analysers. Gas and water purification systems, equipment and filters for reducing emissions, dust collection devices, desulphurisation plant and toxic incinerators are all priorities in the industrial sector, as are recycling and refuse treatment plants for both industrial and household waste. (The Finnish company Rauma Eco Planning is helping in the construction of an installation for processing all types of industrial effluent wastes.)

The Bulgarians are interested in plans to exploit industrial waste as raw materials. For example studies are taking place to process waste to use in brick making where different wastes and ash can be used as plastisers, colouring materials, fluxes, etc.

A growing environmental problem has been the spent fuel from the nuclear reactors at Kozlodui, which the former Soviet Union is no longer prepared to take back without payment in hard currency. The Bulgarian government has recently asked the EC for financial aid to help pay for the building of such a repository, and Western companies are in competition to construct disposal facilities for waste from Kozlodui. British Nuclear Fuels and Comega of France have been helping in the management of the power stations and it is an area where considerable aid funds are available.

MINING AND METALLURGY

Bulgaria has substantial reserves of mainly poor quality brown coal and lignite, some two-thirds of which is open-cast mined in the Maritsa East basin to provide fuel for the Maritsa power station. The total amount of coal mined (mainly lignite) has remained fairly constant over the past 20 years at an annual rate of a little over 30 million tonnes. While investment has continued in this industry by expanding the mines in the Maritsa region, new reserves in the Dobrudzha area remain untapped in spite of feasibility studies conducted by Western companies. Open-cast mining together with the resultant sulphur emissions from coal-powered stations are creating increasing environmental problems.

Bulgaria has limited reserves of lead, although for environmental reasons production at the main plant near Plovdiv has recently been suspended. There are also deposits of copper, zinc, molybdenum, uranium, wolfram, gold and silver.

Deposits of iron ore are comparatively small and of low quality, and the country has been dependent for supply on the USSR. Iron and steel making is largely situated near Sofia, at Pernik, and in a plant built during the late-1980s south-west of Bourgas. Throughout the 1970s and 1980s iron and steel production rose steadily to nearly 10 million tonnes, but in the past few years Bulgaria has failed to achieve its objective of becoming almost self-supporting in most steel products and is currently operating below capacity.

Foreign interest in mining is expected to centre on mining technology, waste removal, anti-pollutant equipment and measuring devices, and the reworking of old mines. In the metallurgy sector investment needs are for technology to reduce energy consumption, anti-pollution and dust equipment, measuring devices, facilities to produce high grade metals (including stainless steel and semimanufactured products), re-equipping of rolling mills, production and repair of mining equipment, casting technology and special steel production capacities.

VEHICLES

Balkancar is the largest fork lift truck manufacturer in the world and has been supplying fork lift trucks to the Soviet Union and other East European countries (it is estimated that there are 600,000 Bulgarian fork lift trucks in the Soviet Union). Balkancar has co-operated with a number of Western companies in production and marketing agreements and will continue to need such assistance if it is to maintain its position as sales to the Eastern bloc countries becomes more difficult.

Madara (Shoumen), now a joint stock company, produces goods vehicles under licence from Skoda as well as axles for the Czecho-slovak market. There are ambitious plans to modernise and enlarge this plant to increase its capacity and range of product. Chavder (Botevgrad) produces some 2500 buses annually with components from Czechoslovakia, Hungary and the UK (Perkins' engines) and is hoping to conclude co-operation agreements with the West. Wamo (Varna) manufactures engines and assembles Moskwitsch cars from Russian CKD kits. Recent joint ventures include an agreement with the Bulgarian motor vehicle electronics industry for major recon-struction of the Volga Motor enterprise at Tolgatti in the Soviet Union to be carried out in co-operation with Fiat. The UK's main venture is Rover's plan to assemble Maestros and this should provide a stimulus for UK component and parts makers. A German company has agreed to co-operate in the building of Ford Pony light duty vans that will be ideal for farmers.

Bulgaria is also a large producer of electric hoists (over 100,000 annually), as well as manufacturing a small number of excavators, bulldozers, tractors and combine harvesters.

Investment opportunities include plant and equipment for the modernisation of factories producing parts and components for vehicles of all kinds, co-operation in diesel engine manufacture and clutches and the introduction into factories of the latest computer management processes.

WOOD AND WOOD PRODUCTS

Bulgaria has large areas of both coniferous and deciduous forests and timber has traditionally been an important sector. Production accounts for 2.5 per cent of total industrial production and the wood and wood products industry employs 63,000 people.

Certain Bulgarian particle boards contain glue not conforming to Western health standards, but an agreement with IKEA of Sweden is designed to remedy this problem and result in the opening up of sales to the West. While output of boards, plywood and veneers has remained steady, the output of the furniture industry grew 3–4 times in the last 20 years (although falling sharply in 1991).

The Bulgarian authorities see the furniture industry as a priority sector and it is an area for licensing and co-operation activity. The industry will, however, need to be far less labour intensive, replace old equipment and improve the quality of its main products including bookcases, wardrobes and office furniture. With good design, these will probably have an increasing market in the West.

Besides needing sorting, sawing, and new electronically controlled processing machines for the timber sector, furniture manufacturers require fire resistant and modern surface lacquering technologies, and universal machines and tools to allow flexible and quick change for small-scale manufacture.

PAPER AND BOARD

The manufacture of cellulose paper and paper products in Bulgaria employs some 18,000 people using mainly indigenous raw material. Paper output was 271,000 tonnes in 1990, of which one-fifth was for printing and 40,000 tonnes for export. Bulgaria plans to increase production which has remained fairly static as increased demand for newsprint, cardboard and paper packaging occurs. Paper mills are situated mainly in the north around Pleven, at Silistra, and near Plovdiv.

Little investment has taken place in this sector in recent years and Western technology will be required, especially for waste processing, chemicals used in manufacturing, together with end-use marketing expertise.

LEATHER, FOOTWEAR, TEXTILES AND CLOTHING

The leather and footwear sectors employ 33,000 people. Production increased steadily throughout the past decade as a result of investment at the main areas of Gabrovo, Lovech, Rousse and

Tolbuhin. There is Western interest generally in the sector, although output fell in 1990 along with most other industries. The sector has seen considerable co-operation activity with Western companies, including footwear, sports and summer wear (Adidas and Puma).

The textiles, knitwear and ready made clothing industries employ nearly 200,000 people, account for 9 per cent of total industrial output of Bulgaria and have been among Bulgaria's leading products. Mills have traditionally been based around Varna, Sofia and Plovdiv.

The industry produces cotton yarn, woollen yarn, cotton fabrics (drawing on an adequate supply of raw materials) and in smaller quantities, silk, hemp and flax fabrics. High investment in the latter half of the 1980s has resulted in better than average performance by these sectors; the textile and knitwear sector being a third higher than in 1980 and ready-made clothing production increasing by more than 50 per cent. Production of clothes remains buoyant, although production of items appealing to the consumer is limited and there is room for improvement in both quality and style. Carpet production, an important industry a few years ago, has suffered dramatically with exports to the former Soviet Union substantially down.

Opportunities in this sector (which is a priority area) include machinery to update the manufacture of such products as wearing apparel, sports and leisure wear, towelling, knitted clothing and hotel linen, children's clothes, plus improved design.

ENGINEERING

Engineering has been the second largest employer in the country. It has a very uncertain future and at the time of writing no clear long-term plans had been laid down. The break up of Comecon resulted in a downturn in output and exports in this sector of nearly 25 per cent in 1990 compared with a year earlier, and 1991 has seen a further fall. Generally, the sector is symptomatic of Bulgaria's industrial problems as a whole: high transport costs, wastages in the use of fuel and labour, lack of management skills, plants requiring modernisation and being made more environmentally friendly, and a traditional overdependence on trade links with the USSR. Many loss-making plants may have to be wound up.

None the less, parts of the sector received very considerable investment under the 5-year plans of the 1980s. NC machine-tools, flexible systems and industrial robots, processing centres, heavy machine building for the mining, power generation, metallurgy and chemical industries, agricultural machinery for fruit, vegetables and tobacco and metal cutting equipment are among the leaders, and it would be expected that the government would make the modernisation of these one of its main priorities.

They will require injections of capital for R&D and management expertise and co-operation with the West if they are to survive in the open market, but all appear to have potential in both export and home markets. Many are central to Bulgaria's plans for modernising its economy, increasing sales in the West and energy generation. Partly through licensing arrangements with the Japanese and as a result of joint production and research co-operation with the USSR, Bulgaria became the world's biggest producer of NC machines and the second largest robot manufacturer. The Bulgarian government has been considering the establishment of joint stock companies with Western partners for the manufacturing enterprises at Bourgas and Rousse, which are to supply equipment to the Russian oil industry. Other areas that seem likely to develop are equipment for the food processing industries, for light industry (leather, footwear and textiles), engineering lines for the service industries, for environmental protection, and for low volume chemical production, plus selected lines for consumer goods that are less research intensive but well designed and made.

CONSTRUCTION MATERIALS AND CERAMICS, TILES AND GLASS

Over 50,000 people are employed in Bulgaria in the manufacture of building materials and a further 22,000 in the manufacture of glass, glass products and fine ceramics.

Production of construction materials showed little change during the 1980s because of relatively low levels of investment and there is a need for the development of new building materials and technologies. The construction industry, an important currency earner especially in the Middle East, has fared a little better and investment enabled activity in this sector to increase by over one-third during the 5 years up to 1991. Bulgaria manufactures some 15 million square metres of plate glass and over 300 million glazed tiles, mainly for export to the former Soviet Union.

Opportunities in this sector should be stimulated by the requirements of the tourist industry, the need for more low-rise, high density housing and improvements in infrastructure.

Bulgaria is to finance viability studies to include modernisation, improved training and the development of export markets for its cement industry, and to find foreign partners and improve management in the six cement plants. In 1990, the largest company at Devnia on the Black Sea produced one-third of Bulgarian total output of 5.5 million tonnes. Priorities will also include joint ventures and the modernisation of old equipment in ceramic wall, floor and roof tile manufacture. New markets will be sought for these products, especially in Western Europe, to replace the former USSR market. In addition, emphasis will be placed on bitumen manufacturing, mineralised thermal insulations, and high technologies for the production of energy saving building materials, prefabricated technologies, and the exploitation of waste in raw materials for brick making and colouring.

Another growth area is expected to be glass production, controlled by Glass and Fine Ceramics in Sofia. At present, production stands at about 15 million square metres per year of building, hardened, reinforced and ornamental glass, U-shaped glass, household glassware and packing glass, mainly at plants at Pernik, Razgrad, Novy Pazar, Pleven, Plovdiv and Elena. The development of the hotel industry and emphasis on the packaging sector for food are expected to stimulate demand.

ELECTRICAL ENGINEERING AND ELECTRONICS

This sector had been the fastest growing and is the largest industrial sector in Bulgaria, employing over half a million people in building electrical and electronic machines and a further 200,000 in the electrotechnical and electronics industries. Throughout the 1980s, it was the recipient of about one-quarter of capital investment in all industries and by 1989 had become the major supplier of magnetic discs and disc drives, control equipment for robots and numerically controlled machines, mainframes and personal computers to the Soviet Union and Comecon countries.

Plants are spread throughout Bulgaria, although nearly a quarter of the industry is situated around Sofia where high performance computer systems (some of them outdated), drive systems, controllers, work stations and silicon components are manufactured. Other important centres include Pravetz (PC boards, personal computers, microprocessors), Veliko Turnovo (VDUs, mini-computers, transformers), Plovdiv (typewriters, printers, computer peripherals and floppy discs), Stara Zagora (a major supplier within Comecon of memory devices, consumer electronics and components), Gabrovo (plotters, digitisers) and Silistra (office equipment).

Bulgaria also has some TV set production (over 200,000 in 1990) and makes a limited number of radios, washing machines, refrigerators, heaters and cash registers.

Bulgaria has been the major supplier of computers and peripherals to Comecon countries and the sector has benefited from co-operation with the West including with Honeywell, Fujitsu, Matra, IBM, Hewlett Packard and Olivetti. While the sector produces some high quality products, insufficient funds are available to carry out the large amount of R&D necessary. Relaxation of CoCom's rules should encourage Western firms interested in this sector. Many firms are facing difficulties as a result of the downturn of the USSR market to which they were geared and the fact that only parts of the industry were IBM compatible. Although they can offer UK companies outlets into the former USSR, the Middle East and North Africa, as well as highly qualified staff, and in many cases (such as the SPS plant) modern equipment, for the main they will require Western investment and new product ranges to ensure their survival.

There appear to be good investment opportunities in component manufacture, control systems, semi-conductor materials, and more sophisticated software, together with improved production of automatic weighing scales, electric meters, lamps, telecommunications equipment and domestic appliances such as microwave ovens, TVs and refrigerators. There is a history of exports of office equipment such as electronic typewriters and calculators, and Bulgaria has capacity available of a high-tech standard to produce a wide variety of PCBs and software packages. The infrastructure exists for Bulgaria to become a major electronic components and parts supplier to the EC and the Far East.

TELECOMMUNICATIONS

Bulgaria has probably the most advanced telecommunications network in Eastern Europe. Its existing infrastructure is mainly analogue and of a design dating back nearly 60 years. It comprises a public switched network, a public telex network and a packet switched network and has developed a comparatively high telephone subscriber density (2.5 million subscribers, or 29 per 100, compared with 14 in 1980). Expansion has been achieved by using obsolete and operationally unreliable equipment together with some capital investment. Bulfax, the fax service introduced in 1988, is steadily improving while telex is still widespread.

BULPAC, the public packet switched data network, provides permanent circuit connections between predefined users and switched circuits for temporary connections between users using the network address system. BULPAC is connected to the German system and is therefore world-wide. A videotex and teletext service are available through BULPAC, but are commercially under-exploited. A mobile telephone system has been installed in Sofia but is costly, while through INFOTEL, experiments in access to information, electronic mail and teletext are taking place. GPT, owned by GEC/Siemens, has agreed a joint venture with the Committee for Posts and Telecommunications and Informatics to create BETKOM which has installed card-operated payphones at business and holiday centres in Bulgaria. The Committee has recommended a number of proposals to improve telecommunications in Bulgaria, including restructuring the service for which a small amount of EEC aid has been made available, and the introduction of new technology.

The changes envisaged include the construction of a digital network and trunk overlay network using fibre optics and the microwave system, followed by a cellular network mainly covering Sofia and Plovdiv, a packet switching data-transmission network for business and videotex for smaller companies. State monopoly over radio and TV has already been removed on a regional basis but not (to date) nationally. Future development is seen in the provision of new high powered, long wave radio transmitters, equipment for stereophonic transmission and relay stations. At the end of 1990, there were 85 radio transmitters, 68 TV transmitters and nearly 1000 relay stations.

TRANSPORT INFRASTRUCTURE

The sector benefited from heavy investment throughout the 1980s, but will need to be given priority if the country is to develop tourism and its trade links with the West. Bulgaria is situated at the crossroads between Europe and the Middle East and five years ago was able to claim that SO-MAT, the International Road Transport Economic Corporation, was Europe's largest road haulier carrying in 1986 nearly one billion tonnes of freight (although by 1990 this figure had fallen to a quarter of a billion).

While some roads have been improved in recent years, they have tended to be more orientated towards trade with the Soviet Union (such as the road between Sofia, Varna and Bourgas) and to a lesser extent with the Middle East. To facilitate trade with the West, and with the Middle East, the Bulgarians are planning to complete 70 kilometres of the Trakya motorway – part of the Trans European Motorway (North–South TEM). The Bulgarians are looking to international investment for road projects including the construction of an orbital road around Sofia. One idea being considered is to build privatised motorways whereby the return on the private capital invested is for a given period, secured through tolls.

Bulgaria has a rail network of some 6600 kilometres, nearly two-thirds of which is electrified. Freight carried by rail represents less than 20 per cent of the total carried and has also fallen sharply to less than it was in 1970. The government has decided to continue work on the Sofia underground and planned to provide Lev60 million in 1991, plus Lev325 million and Lev150 million in 1992 and 1993 respectively. The rail network is in need, however, of automotive management systems, mechanical loading facilities and containerisation.

The international airports have suffered from lack of long-term investment and consideration is being given to building a new airport at Sofia. Bulgaria has recently leased modern Boeings and Airbuses from the West to replace the older fleet of Russian Antonovs and Tupolevs. The number of services has fallen with the number of visitors from the Soviet Union and Eastern Europe drying up, coupled with the quadrupling in the price of fuel. The long-term prospects are brighter, however, with joint ventures with Singapore, Italy and Austria under discussion, as well as agreements under consideration with Lufthansa, Air France, Swiss Air, British Aerospace and others on the managing and running of airports and airlines.

There are 34 million kilometres of paved roads (3 million unpaved) which carry the bulk of traffic. About 6 per cent of Bulgaria's trade is by sea and there are nearly 2 million tonnes deadweight of ships under the Bulgarian flag, including 100,000 tonnes tankers and container vessels. Varna to Odessa is an important ferry link in trading with the former Soviet Union.

RESEARCH AND TECHNOLOGY

In 1990, 3 per cent of national income was devoted to R&D (compared with 2.3 per cent 10 years earlier) – a proportion that the government aims to increase. There are some 500 scientific and engineering organisations and institutions in Bulgaria, the most important being the Bulgarian Academy of Sciences, the Agricultural Academy and the Medical Academy. Over 31,000 people are classified as scientific workers covering technical medical, natural, agricultural and social sciences – half as many again as in 1980.

Priority in recent years has been for research into electronics, robotics (particularly for machine tools), biotechnical and chemical studies, transport systems based on electronics, new raw and prime materials, laser techniques and optoelectronics. Much of the work undertaken has been with firm government control and in close co-operation with the former Soviet Union and other Comecon countries.

The previous system produced a large number of well-educated graduates (in 1990, it had 300,000 higher education graduates and nearly 750,000 secondary graduates out of a work-force of some 4 million).

Bulgaria must now look towards the West for co-operation in scientific research and is one of the countries benefiting from the Tempus, JIPAC and other schemes whereby training can be given to Bulgarian teachers and students in technical organisations and companies in the West. Projects included in the schemes cover engineering, business management and applied sciences.

SERVICES

Along with other East European countries, the service sector in Bulgaria had been neglected largely for ideological reasons. It is an area, however, where UK companies have done very well in other parts of Eastern Europe. The most immediate requirement is for Western professional advice especially in creating the infrastructure for a market economy and (in the wake of the privatisation proposals involving the development of sector plans) management consultancy, expertise in financial services, banking, insurance and accountancy. Assistance for the financial sector and banking is the second largest aid sector after energy/environment. Financial assistance for training and development and human resources are also available through the Know-How Fund and the World Bank.

We would expect to see a wide range of opportunities for other services. For example, the establishment of new distribution systems to cope with the rise in consumer demand, property and architectural services, quantity surveyors, environmental, freight forwarding and transport consultants and education services connected to the tourist industry (such as restaurant and hotel management, renovation and promotion of historical monuments). The country may also benefit from an input of designers for consumer goods, although there is some local talent in this field, including, for example, the Nery partnership. The media, including newspaper production (the first new national independent daily newspaper was launched by Megapress early in 1992), local TV and communication services will offer increasing outlets for Western advertising, publishing, printing and related services.

Appendix 2

Sources of Grants and Aid

Although Bulgaria was a late starter, its move towards a Western style market economy has been highly appreciated by the international community. The far reaching economic reform programme was drawn up in close co-operation with the IMF and the World Bank.

Bulgarian reform efforts are being supported by the international financial community, (the IMF, the World Bank, the EC and the Group of 24) through the revival of external financing. The framework of financial support that has already been granted to Bulgaria comprises:

- a 12-month stand-by credit of SDR279 million in 1991;

- a 12-month stand-by credit of SDR155 million in 1992;

- a credit of SDR93.2 million under CCFF of the IMF in 1991;

- a US$250 million structural adjustment loan from the World Bank (a US$150 million tranche in 1991 and US$100 million in 1992);

- a US$17 million technical assistance loan from the World Bank in 1992; and

- US$400 million in medium and long-term credits received from the EC/Group of 24. The allocation of the European Community's share of ECU290 million was agreed in June 1991.

The stand-by credits granted by the IMF are aimed at supporting the current balance of payments position.

The credits like structural adjustment loans and those from the EC/Group of 24 have been granted in support of the structural reform efforts of the Bulgarian government. They will be attributed on condition that certain commitments are fulfilled by Bulgaria in respect of the restructuring of the economy and the restaggering of debt.

The SAL is foreseen to be of extreme importance for future economic reforms. The loan has an aggregate value equivalent to US$250 million and has been granted for 17 years, including a 5-year grace period. The interest rate is floating. Interest is payable on the principal amount of the outstanding loan at a rate for each interest period equal to the cost of qualified borrowing determined in respect of the preceding semester, plus one-half of one per cent. The interest period is six months.

SAL will be granted in two tranches. The first US$150 million tranche was granted for the disposal of the Bulgarian government. Agreement was reached with the IMF and the World Bank that the first tranche should be used for oil imports. The second tranche will be released to Bulgaria under the following conditions:

- to enact a privatisation law and adopt a programme for privatisation of selected large state enterprises in 1992;

- to adopt a debt strategy consistent with the macroeconomic framework;

- to continue satisfactory progress in carrying out the privatisation of land available for cultivation;

- to improve the organisation, management and operation of state-owned enterprises; and

- to carry out the programme for the restructuring and consolidation of banks.

PHARE funds committed to Bulgaria in 1990–91 were as follows:

- ECU16 million for support of the agricultural reform;

- ECU5 million for improvement of mother and child care;

- ECU3.5 million for environmental monitoring;

- ECU5 million for medical equipment;

- ECU3 million for telecommunications; and

- ECU3 million for telecommunications.

PHARE funds committed to Bulgaria for 1991–92 are as follows

- ECU20 million for private sector promotion;

- ECU15 million for financial and economic infrastructure;
- ECU25 million for the agricultural sector; and
- ECU3 million for telecommunications.

Appendix 3

Bibliography and Sources of Further Information

BIBLIOGRAPHY

Books

Bulgaria: The Business Handbook, DRT Europe Services, Brussels, May 1992.

East Central Europe Between the Two World Wars, Joseph Rothschild, University of Washington Press, vol IX, 1990.

A Short History of Modern Bulgaria, R J Crampton, Cambridge University Press, 1986.

Surge To Freedom, J F Brown, Duke University Press, 1991.

Periodicals and Journals

Accountancy Act – National Chart of Accounts (in English), Ministry of Finance and Deloitte Touche Tohmatsu International, Sofia, May 1992.

Business Eastern Europe, weekly, Business International Ltd, London.

Bulgarian Business News (168 Hours), weekly, Bulgarian Business News, Sofia.

Bulgarian Country Report – International Risk and Payment Review, Dun & Bradstreet, High Wycombe.

Bulgarian Economic Outlook, monthly, The Bulgarian News Agency, Sofia.

Business Visa For You, monthly, Bulgarian Chamber of Commerce and Industry, VEZNI Information and Publishing House, Sofia.

Central European Magazine, monthly, Euromoney Publications, London.

The Continent, daily (newspaper), Megapress, Sofia (UK contact: Cerrex Ltd, National House, Wardour Street, London W1V 3HP).

East European Investment Monthly, monthly, Dixon & Company, New York.

East West, fortnightly report, East West Sprl, Belgium.

The Eastern European Newsletter, fortnightly, Eastern European Newsletter, London.

The Economist Intelligence Unit Reports, quarterly, The Economist Intelligence Unit, London.

Financial Times East European Business Law, monthly, Financial Times Business Information Ltd, London.

Financial Times Eastern European Markets, fortnightly, Financial Times Business Information Ltd, London.

Insight (Eastern European Business Report), monthly, Insight International Publishing, London.

'International Markets' in *London Commerce*, London Chamber of Commerce and Industry, London.

Plan Econ, fortnightly, Plan Econ Europe Ltd, London.

Summary of World Broadcasts, weekly economic reports, Eastern Europe BBC Monitoring Service, Reading.

Technical Assistance/Critical Imports Loan, World Bank Appraisal Report, London, June 1991.

SOURCES OF FURTHER INFORMATION

Archibald Campbell
Deloitte and Touche Eastern
    Europe Liaison
Touche Ross & Co*
Hill House
1 Little New St
London EC4A 3TR
Tel: 071-936 3000
Fax: 071-583 8517
*For additional services, please contact the following at the above address:
Auditing and Accounting:
    Nigel Johnson
Taxation: Peter Parsons/Paul
    Glover

Touche Ross & Co
Peterborough Court
133 Fleet Street
London EC4A 2TR
Tel: 071-936 3000
Fax: 071-583 1198
For further specialist services, please contact the following at the above address:
Environmental Audit: Ken
    Beecham
Management Consultancy: Brian
    Pomeroy/Stuart Mungall
Tourism and Hotels: Graham
    Wason

For *Corporate Finance* services,
    please contact:
Martin Clarke/David Douglas
Touche Ross & Co
Friary Court
65 Crutched Friars
London EC3N 2NP
Tel: 071-936 3000
Fax: 071-480 6958

Vasko Raichev/Ilian Petrov
Deloitte & Touche
17 Benkovski Street
1000 Sofia
Bulgaria
Tel/Fax: 010 359 2 81 07 29
Fax: 010 359 2 81 07 43

Sinclair Roche & Temperley *
Broadwalk House
5 Appold St
London EC2A 2NN
Tel: 071-638 9044
Fax: 071-638 0354
* For a range of specialist services,
please contact the following at the
above address:
Legal: Ian Gaunt, Richard Thomas,
    Campbell Steedman
Corporate Finance: Richard
    Thomas, Campbell Steedman
Environmental Audit: Richard
    Buxton, Gerard Hopkins
Taxation: David Relf

Frank Hancock
SG Warburg & Co
1 Finsbury Avenue
London EC2M 2PA
Tel: 071-606 1066
Fax: 071-382 4800

Michael Bird/R A H Tucker
Cerrex Ltd
6th Floor
National House
60–66 Wardour Street
London W1V 3HP
Tel: 071-734 2879
Fax: 0923 858013

Barbara Page Roberts
PR Trading
The Old White Hart
113 High St
Odiham
Hampshire RG25 1LA
Tel: 0256 703621
Fax: 0256 704059

Brian Cole
East European Projects
    Consultants
Drake Wood
Devonshire Avenue
Amersham
Bucks HP6 5JF
Tel: 0494 726281
Fax: 0494 432281

Margarit Todorov
Managing Director
Domaine Boyar
12 Alphabet Works
Hawgood St
London E3 3RU
Tel: 071-537 3707
Fax: 071-537 9377

Peter Schwarz
Exploration manager, UK and
    Europe
British Gas
100 Thames Valley Park Drive
Reading
Berkshire RG16 1PT
Tel: 0734 292015
Fax: 0734 292027

Rod Allen
Country manager, Bulgaria
ICL
ICL House
1 High St
Putney
London SW15 1SW
Tel: 081-788 7272
Fax: 081-565 6625

David Nutton
Senior Marketing Manager
Racal Recorders Ltd
Hardley Industrial Estate
Hythe
Southampton
Hampshire SO4 6ZH
Tel: 0703 843265
Fax: 0703 848919

Valentin Braykov
Braykov's Legal Office
Bl 15 Dimiter Manov St
12th Floor, Apartment 43
1408 Sofia

Keith Welford
Department of Trade and Industry
66–74 Victoria St
London SW1H 0ET
Tel: 071-215 5302
Fax: 071-222 2531
Telex: 8813148

Confederation of British Industry
Initiative Eastern Europe
Centre Point
103 New Oxford Street
London WC1A 1DU
Tel: 071-379 7400
Fax: 071-240 1578
Telex: 21332

London Chamber of Commerce
and Industry
69 Cannon Street
London EC4N 5AB
Tel: 071-248 4444
Fax: 071-489 0391
Telex: 888941

British Bulgarian Chamber of
Commerce
c/o The Commercial Department
The Bulgarian Embassy
186–88 Queen's Gate
London SW7 5HL
Tel: 071-584 9400
Fax: 071-584 4948

Ivan Stancioff
Ambassador
Embassy of the Republic of
Bulgaria
186–88 Queen's Gate
London SW7 5HL
Tel: 071-584 9400
Fax: 071-581 3244

John Wilton
World Bank Trade Centre
1057 Sofia
Fax: 010 359 2 770 006

European Bank for Reconstruction
and Development
One Exchange Square
London EC2A 2EH
Tel: 071-338 6000
Fax: 071-338 6100

Pierre-Yves Divisia
Senior Banker
Merchant Banking
(as above)
Tel: 071-338 6165

Christian Schmidt
Acting Country Manager
Development Banking
(as above)
Tel: 071-338 6389

Mrs Lea Cohen
Ambassador
Mission of the Republic of Bulgaria
  to the EC
av Moscicki 7
1180 Bruxelles
Tel: 010 32 2 374 84 68
Fax: 010 32 2 374 91 84

Christine Hughes
EC co-ordinator of PHARE for
  Bulgaria
DG-1
86 Rue de la Loi
B-1049 Brussels
Belgium
Tel: 010 32 2 23 58511

Plamen Gogov
PHARE co-ordination officer
  Ministry of Finance
102 Rakovski Str
1040 Sofia
Tel: 010 359 2 86 92 19
     010 359 2 88 59 46
Fax: 010 359 2 87 26 01

Geoff Leader
Know-How Fund
Joint Assistance Unit
Foreign and Commonwealth Office
Old Admiralty Building
London SW1A 2AF
Tel: 071-210 1418

Reinhard Thomas
EC Commission
Rue de la Loi 200
B-1049 Brussels
Belgium
Tel: 010 32 2 23 54707/51542
Fax: 010 32 2 23 63308

David Stokes
British Council
Director
7 Tulovo St
1504 Sofia
Tel: 010 359 2 44 33 94
Fax: 010 359 2 46 20 65

EC TEMPUS Office
Bd Aleksander Stamboliiski 18
BG-1000 Sofia
Tel: 010 359 2 88 49 74
Fax: 010 359 2 88 49 74

Thomas O'Sullivan
EC representative
The Sheraton
5 Sveta Nedel Sq
1000 Sofia
Tel: 010 359 2 87 10 38
Fax: 010 359 2 87 65 41

John Northover
First Secretary Commercial
British Embassy
Boulevard Marshal Tolbukhin
    65–67
Sofia
Tel: 010 359 2 88 53 61
Fax: 010 359 2 65 60 22

American Embassy
1 Stamboliysky Blvd
1000 Sofia
Tel: 010 359 2 884 801/5

PHARE Project Management Units in Bulgaria

The environment
Dimitar Vodenitcharov
Minister of Environment
Director
Vladimir Poptomov St 67
1000 Sofia
Tel: 010 359 2 87 61 51
Fax: 010 359 2 52 16 34

Development of SMEs
Vera Hristova
Co-ordinator
and
Herbert van Werkhoven
External expert
Ministry of Industry, Trade and
  Service
29 Aksakov Street
1046 Sofia
Tel: 010 359 2 87 19 13
Fax: 010 359 2 87 19 12

Telecommunications
Svetoslav Tinchev
Director
PTT-Ministry
6 Gourko Str
1000 Sofia
Tel: 010 359 2 87 18 37
Fax: 010 359 2 80 25 80

Agriculture
Stewart Campbell
Director
Project Management Unit,
  Agriculture
Ministry of Foreign Economic
  Relations
Graf Ignatiev St 10
Sofia
Tel: 010 359 2 80 24 15
Fax: 010 359 2 87 16 23

*Enterprise restructuring and
  privatisation*
Vera Hristova
Coordinator
and
José M Lloveras and John Mitchell
External experts
Ministry of Industry, Trade and
  Service
29 Aksakov Str
1046 Sofia
Tel: 010 359 2 87 19 14
Fax: 010 359 2 87 19 15

Health
Mrs Milena Kantardjieva
Director
Ministry of Health
Sveta Nedelia Square 5
1000 Sofia
Tel: 010 359 2 87 44 40
Fax: 010 359 2 80 00 31

Nuclear safety
Mr Radulov
Director
and
Mr R Petit
Project Manager
External expert
Emergency Programme
Nuclear Safety Committee of
  Energy
8 Tridiza Street
1040 Sofia
Tel: 010 359 2 88 43 92
Fax: 010 359 2 87 58 26

Energy
Mr Radulov
Director
Triaditza St 8
1040 Sofia
Tel: 010 359 2 86 191
Fax: 010 359 2 80 11 48

Bulgarian Chamber of Commerce
  and Industry
11A A Stamboliiski Blvd
1000 Sofia
Tel: 010 359 2 87 26 31
Fax: 010 359 2 87 32 09
Telex: 2237474

Scientific Institute for
    International Cooperation and
    Foreign Economic Activities
3A 165 Str
zh k Izgreva
1113 Sofia
Tel: 010 359 2 70 83 36
Fax: 010 359 2 70 51 54
Telex: 22271

Bulgarian Industrial Assocation
14 Alabin Str
1000 Sofia
Tel: 010 359 2 87 96 11
Fax: 010 359 2 87 26 04
Telex: 23523

Interpred World Trade Centre
D Zankov Blvd
1057 Sofia
Tel: 010 359 2 71 46 46
Fax: 010 359 2 70 00 04
Telex: 023284

Institute for the Development of
    Industry
12A Ho Chi Min Blvd
1592 Sofia
Tel: 010 359 2 79 00 04
Fax: 010 359 2 79 91 34
Telex: 22011

Institute of Marketing
2 K Shapkarov ul
1330 Sofia
Tel: 010 359 2 20 69 65
Fax: 010 359 2 23 10 83

New Technology Association
4 Arch Milanov ul
1000 Sofia
Tel: 010 359 2 65 50 91
Fax: 010 359 2 66 19 73

Central Institute for Software
    Products and Systems
52 G M Dimitrov Blvd
1040 Sofia
Tel: 010 359 2 71 20 24
Fax: 010 359 2 71 01 57
Telex: 22404

Ministry of Foreign Affairs
2 Al Zhendov Str
1113 Sofia
Tel: 010 359 2 71 43 1
Fax: 010 359 2 70 05 36
Telex: 865 22529

Ministry of Agriculture
55 Khr Botev Blvd
1040 Sofia
Tel: 010 359 2 85 31
Fax: 010 359 2 80 06 55
Telex: 865 22325

Ministry of Finance
102 Rakovski Str
1000 Sofia
Tel: 010 359 2 87 06 22
Fax: 010 359 2 80 11 48
Telex: 865 22727

Ministry of Industry and Trade
8 Slavyanska Str
1000 Sofia
Tel: 010 359 2 87 07 41
Fax: 010 359 2 89 76 05
Telex: 865 23490

Ministry of Transport
9 Levski Srt
1000 Sofia
Tel: 010 359 2 88 12 30
Fax: 010 359 2 88 50 94
Telex: 865 23200

Ministry of Regional Development,
 Homebuilding Policy and
 Construction
17–19 Kiril i Metodiy Str
1000 Sofia
Tel: 010 359 2 83 84 1
Fax: 010 359 2 87 25 17
Telex: 865 22182

Ministry of Education and Science
18 Stamboliysky blvd
1000 Sofia
Tel: 010 359 2 83 85 1
Fax: 010 359 2 87 12 89
Telex: 865 22384

Ministry of Justice
2 Dondukov blvd
1000 Sofia
Tel: 010 359 2 86 01
Fax: 010 359 2 867 32 26
Telex: 865 22933

Ministry of Health
5 Sv Nedelia Sq
1000 Sofia
Tel: 010 359 2 86 31
Fax: 010 359 2 80 00 31
Telex: 865 23654

Ministry of Labour and Social
 Affairs
2 Trijadiza Str
1000 Sofia
Tel: 010 359 2 86 01
Fax: 010 359 2 80 06 09
Telex: 865 23173

Ministry of Culture
17 Stamboliysky blvd
1000 Sofia
Tel: 010 359 2 86 11 1
Fax: 010 359 2 87 73 39
Telex: 865 22652

Ministry of Environment
67 William Gladston Str
1000 Sofia
Tel: 010 359 2 87 61 51
Fax: 010 359 2 52 16 34
Telex: 865 22145

Ministry of Defence
1 Aksakov Str
1000 Sofia
Tel: 010 359 2 54 60 01
Fax: 010 359 2 862 45 36

Committee of Communications
 and Information
6 Gurko Str
1000 Sofia
Tel: 010 359 2 88 20 95
Fax: 010 359 2 80 25 80
Telex: 865 22515

Committee for Geology and
 Mineral Resources
22 Kniaginia Maria Louisa Blvd
1000 Sofia
Tel: 010 359 2 83 85 1
Fax: 010 359 2 83 35 68
Telex: 865 22502

Committee for Energy
8 Triaditsa Str
1000 Sofia
Tel: 010 359 2 86 19 1
Fax: 010 359 2 87 58 26
Telex: 865 22707

Committee for Tourism
1 Sv Nedelia Sq
1000 Sofia
Tel: 010 359 2 84 13 1
Fax: 010 359 2 88 20 66
Telex: 865 23553

Committee for Standardization,
Certification and Metrology
21 6-ti Septemvri Str
1000 Sofia
Tel: 010 359 2 85 91
Fax: 010 359 2 80 14 02
Telex: 865 22570

Foreign Help Agency
2 Dondukov Blvd
1123 Sofia
Tel: 010 359 2 85 01 ext 2226

Privatisation Agency
10A Graf Ignatiev Str
1000 Sofia
Tel: 010 359 2 88 21 22
Fax: 010 359 2 88 06 05

National Statistical Institute
2 Panaiot Volov Str
1504 Sofia
Tel: 010 359 2 43 40 1

Bulgarian Telegraph Agency
49 Tsarigradsko shausse Blvd
1504 Sofia
Tel: 010 359 2 85 61
Telex: 865 22587

BTPP
Bulgarian Chamber of Commerce
and Industry
11A Al Stamboliysky Blvd
1000 Sofia
Tel: 010 359 2 87 26 31
Fax: 010 359 2 87 32 09
Telex: 865 22374

Bulgarian Industrial Camara
14 Alabin Str
1000 Sofia
Tel: 010 359 2 84 11
Fax: 010 359 2 87 26 04
Telex: 865 23523

Jusautor Copyright Agency
11 Slaveikov Str
1000 Sofia
POB 872
Tel: 010 359 2 87 91 11

Sofia Press Agency
29 Slavyanska Str
1040 Sofia
Tel: 010 359 2 88 58 31
Telex: 865 22622

International Plovdiv Fair
37 Vazrajdane Blvd
4018 Plovdiv
Tel: 010 359 32 56 29
Fax: 010 359 32 26 54 32
Telex: 865 44432

Union for Citizens' Economic
Initiatives
2A Al Stamboliysky Blvd
1000 Sofia
Tel: 010 359 2 86 81

Private Producers Union
2 T Kableshkov Str
1000 Sofia
Tel: 010 359 2 55 00 16

Union of Small and Medium-Size
Enterprises
14 Ekzarkh Yossif Str
1000 Sofia
Tel: 010 359 2 84 21

Scientific Institute for
International Cooperation and
Foreign Economy
3A 165 Str
1113 Sofia, j k Izgreva
Tel: 010 359 2 70 83 35
Fax: 010 359 2 70 01 31
Telex: 865 22271

Bulgarian National Bank
1 Kniaz Al Batenberg Sq
1000 Sofia
Tel: 010 359 2 85 51
Fax: 010 359 2 88 05 58
Telex: 865 22392

Bulgarian Foreign Trade Bank
1 Kniaz Al Batenberg Sq
1000 Sofia
Tel: 010 359 2 85 51
Telex: 865 22031

State Savings Bank
19 Moskovska Str
1040 Sofia
Tel: 010 359 2 88 10 41
Telex: 865 22719

Mineralbank
17 Legue Str
1000 Sofia
Tel: 010 359 2 80 17 37
Telex: 865 23390

Agricultural and Cooperative Bank
37 Vazrajdane Blvd
4018 Plovdiv
Tel: 010 359 32 23 18 76
Fax: 010 359 32 83 52 23
Telex: 865 44324

Biochim
1 Ivan Vazov Str
1000 Sofia
Tel: 010 359 2 54 13 66
Fax: 010 359 2 54 13 78
Telex: 865 23862

Stroybank
46 Dunav Str
1000 Sofia
Tel: 010 359 2 83 84 1
Fax: 010 359 2 83 52 23
Telex: 865 23887

Economic Bank
8 Slavyanska Str
1000 Sofia
Tel: 010 359 2 87 07 41
Fax: 010 359 2 88 55 26
Telex: 865 23910

Elektronika Bank
55 Chapaev Str
1574 Sofia
Tel: 010 359 2 73 55 1
Fax: 010 359 2 88 54 67
Telex: 865 23789

Bank for Agricultural Credits
55 Khristo Botev Blvd
1606 Sofia
Tel: 010 359 2 85 31
Fax: 010 359 2 51 07 45
Telex: 865 24470

1st Private Bank
2A Stambolijski Blvd
1000 Sofia
Tel: 010 359 2 87 20 47
Fax: 010 359 2 65 93 88
Telex: 865 24540

Tourist-Sport Bank
18 Vassil Levski Blvd
1000 Sofia
Tel: 010 359 2 83 28 56
Fax: 010 359 2 88 31 30
Telex: 865 24722

Index